Cockfidence

The Extraordinary Lover's
Guide To Being The Man
You Want To Be And Driving
Women Wild

Celeste Hirschman, M.A.
Danielle Harel, Ph.D.

Somatica Press

COCKFIDENCE
By Celeste Hirschman, MA and Danielle Harel, PhD

www.CelesteAndDanielle.com

Published by Somatica Press

Cover design: Yair Harel

Cover photos: Tiffany Schoepp
www.TiffPhoto.com

Interior design: Joel Friedlander
www.theBookDesigner.com

This book is not intended as a substitute for the medical advice
of physicians. The reader should regularly consult a physician in
matters relating to his/her health and particularly with respect to
any symptoms that may require diagnosis or medical attention.

ISBN 978-0-9832403-0-3
Printed in the United States of America
First Edition

Somatica Press

Acknowledgments

There are so many people walking around with books inside them, and we realize we are among the extraordinarily fortunate because we have had a whole team working with us to bring *Cockfidence* to fruition. We could never have done this without the loving support and constant help and feedback of Yair Harel and Dimitry Yakoushkin – thank you for bringing your creativity, enthusiasm and commitment to the project. A big, heartfelt thanks to Rich Friesen, who sat with us for long hours recording our babblings and gave feedback on drafts. Warm hugs and thanks to our editing heroes: thank you David Lazarony, Ed Bierman, David H., Matt Schindler, Jon Hull, Chris Ward, Marty Friesen, and Tom Rehor. Great big hugs of gratitude to Celeste's family: her mom, Magick, for hosting weekend writing marathons and content brainstorms; her sister, Allegra, for her socially conscious edits and witty contributions; her sister, April, who always keeps the dream alive and reminded us to take care of ourselves in the process and her father, Marc, who read to her nightly as a child and had more books in the house than the local library. Thank you to Danielle's children, Sitar and Shiraz, who are teaching her about love every day. Huge appreciations to our content editor, Laura Cross, with her stunning eye for organization and much-needed encouragements. Finally, a tremendous thank you to all of our clients and workshop participants – in every moment we have spent with you, we have learned and loved, laughed and cried and co-created a more passionate, expressive, and dynamic world in which to live.

Table of Contents

Start Here

There is nothing like the power you feel when you bring a woman to a place where she is hot, inviting and generous with her sexuality, you make her scream with orgasms and she wants more and more. What you might not realize is that most women have this capacity, but it takes a confident, erotically powerful and skilled lover to encourage a woman towards her full sexual potential. You can be this confident, powerful, virile man and be an Extraordinary Lover. You can have passionate, satisfying and exciting sex and relationships with amazing women. You can be this man all the time.

In our practice, we meet men who want to be themselves and understand what women want sexually and interpersonally. We have so much compassion for men; men and women are very different and it can be very confusing to try to figure out what women want. In the process of connecting with women, there are many stumbling blocks that may pull you out of your center.

These include hiding your sexual desire for fear of rejection; misunderstanding women, their emotions and their desires; or fearing that connecting with a woman in any way means making a commitment, even if you aren't ready.

There is an art to becoming the kind of man who claims his own desires *and* satisfies a woman's deepest longings. This book teaches you the secret connection between stepping into your power and igniting a woman's desire. The secret is found in your connection with your sexual energy and we call this connection *Cockfidence*.

Throughout your life, you've probably met men who seem to just have it; they get all the women while doing whatever they want to do. You may think *Cockfidence* is something that people either have naturally or don't. *Cockfience* is actually a set of qualities that can be developed.

We have worked with thousands of men and women, both single and in relationship, and we have discovered that *Cockfidence* is built from nine personal qualities.

We call these the 9 Qualities of an Extraordinary Lover:

1. Presence
2. Acceptance
3. Confidence
4. Generosity
5. Passion

6. Empathy
7. Curiosity
8. Spontaneity
9. Sensuality

Using these 9 Qualities, we developed a transformative process that has changed the lives and relationships of our clients. In this book, we reveal our secrets and walk you through all that we have discovered so you too can become a *Cockfident* man.

This book is for all men whether single, dating, in a relationship or married; it also for all women who want to support the men in their lives and learn about their own sexuality. For a man who is single or dating, *Cockfidence* means you approach women with ease and playfulness and attract them with sincerity, not deception. You are also confident in your sexual desire and know you've got what it takes to please them sexually. For men in a new relationship, *Cockfidence* means knowing your partner wants you. You also know how to create a safe space where your partner can open up to you and give all of herself, sexually and emotionally. For men in long-term relationship or married men, *Cockfidence* means that, once the honeymoon period is over and the hormones are fading, you know how to keep seduction and creativity alive. You also leave room for growth and change in your sex life and your relationship. Finally, this book is for women who want to better understand themselves and their partner and support him in growing his *Cockfidence*.

Whether single or in a relationship you need to bring your *Cockfidence* everywhere you go – from the bedroom to the boardroom. This does not mean that you want to flirt or have sex with every woman you meet; it means that you make the choice where you direct this energy. As you develop your *Cockfidence*, it is also important to stay within the agreements you've made with your partner or partners. Unfortunately, the message that men get in our culture is that staying within your agreements means shutting your erotic energy down except when you are with your partner. In the long run, this creates blocks to your desire and your overall motivation and enjoyment of life. Remaining open to your erotic energy is a large part of what keeps you succeeding in your relationship and in the world.

We have to admit we have a selfish reason for writing this book. As empowered sexual women, we want to live in a world full of men who can express their power and passion, who bring their *Cockfidence* and meet us fully. We believe many women make themselves small to protect their partners, but when they have an empowered *Cockfident* man, they can allow themselves to open sexually and emotionally with a partner who can receive them fully.

We want to let you in on a big secret. Very few women will tell you that they are excited by men who live their lives from their own desires and passions because they are also frightened of it. It is exactly this slightly unsettled feeling that causes women to respect, desire and want to fuck you over and over again. Complete certainty that you will do what they expect you to do may give women a false sense of security, but it also breeds boredom and contempt. Women's excitement is inspired by your tenacious commitment to who you are and what you want.

Through our workshops and private practice as sex and relationship therapists, we have learned a lot about women and supported men in offering women what they *really* want while staying true to themselves. Our work is practical, experiential and body-based. Everything we teach is about taking action and creating real change in your life. Our experiential, body-based approach makes change happen quickly. Sexual desire, pleasure and attraction do not happen only in the brain; sexual connection takes skills and awareness that only happen when you directly engage the body.

Imagine trying to learn baseball or the guitar through talking, without ever practicing your swing or your chords. You would never be able to play. Until you practice how to be present, passionate and sensual, nothing much changes in your sex life and relationships. You don't get to *really* play! This book is a practical, step-by-step guide to connect you with your own *Cockfidence* and see real change in your sex life and relationships. We congratulate you for beginning your *Cockfidence* journey now!

How to Use This Book

The best way to use this book is to take it chapter by chapter, completing the exercises as you go and letting each chapter take time to sink in as you create new patterns in your life. This book is largely about breaking old habits and making room for your unique style and attractiveness to come through. Many of these things will be new to you, remember to bring an open mind and give yourself the gift of patience and support as you continue on your journey.

This book is divided into two sections and organized by the 9 Qualities of an Extraordinary Lover. The first section is about being the man you want to be by finding your own authentic version of masculinity, magnetism and power. It includes the qualities of presence, acceptance, confidence, generosity and passion. In order to live your life fully, it is essential to be present in your experiences; feel acceptance for yourself and your partner(s); feel confident in your desires and abilities; give generously but within your boundaries; and come to your life and relationships with passionate intensity. It is essential to do the work inside yourself before you can have hot, authentic connections with women.

The second section is about driving women wild, understanding who they are, what they want and how you can give them what they want without losing your own center and clarity. In this section we cover the qualities of empathy, curiosity, spontaneity and sensuality. In order to ignite a woman's sexual desire and attraction, you need to respond skillfully to her emotions and be open and curious about her. It is essential to bring your own creative, sensual approach and be flexible in the face of her changing needs, moods and desires. In this section we bring in practical tools, breaking down each of these qualities so that you can embody them in your connections with women. If you follow the steps in both parts of this book you will create the sex life and the relationships you want!

By embodying these qualities you can be the kind of man women desire and other men admire. You become the sexy, confident man you were always meant to be and move beyond all that has been blocking you. The 9 Qualities of an Extraordinary Lover are the pathway to *Cockfidence*; you discover your own desires and women's deepest longings and create a life where your desires and her longings can be actualized.

This is a hero's journey. It is about living your own truth and it requires bravery, perseverance, and the willingness to take risks and try something new.

If there is anything we have learned from our work with men, it is that all men have this hero inside of them. He is not a hero who saves damsels in distress, he is a hero who meets women with his own power. He is connected to himself and creates a space where women can feel their strength and sensuality. We know that you have this hero deep inside of you and we invite you to enjoy the ride as you bring him out into the world!

Be The Man
You Want To Be

Presence

Presence is being fully and completely in the moment, staying connected with yourself, and bringing all of your attention and intention to whatever experience you are having. It is the simple sentence, "I am here with you, open to all that you are, and I don't need to change anything about myself." In this sentence, the "I" comes first and, to come into presence, you must get in touch with yourself first.

So take a moment and ask yourself, "Who the hell am I and what do I want?" Good. Now *don't think* about your answer. Most people try to answer this question from their head. If you try to answer this question with your head, you will be right where most of us are most of the time, lost in thought and disconnected from your body and your real desires. Unfortunately, your head lies to you many times a day, saying things like, "You should be more successful," or "It's inappropriate to check out the cute girl in the next aisle at the grocery store." On the other hand, when we listen to our bodies and emotions, we hear our deeper truth. In order to know what you want and feel powerful, you first need to come into connection with this deeper knowing in your body.

By connecting to your body, you feel your sense of who you are and your personal power. Personal power is not power over anyone – it is power in relationship with everyone. To feel powerful, you do not need to be in charge of other people and you don't need people to cower in front of you. What you need is to know yourself fully, accept yourself unapologetically and bring this kind of presence no matter who is standing in front of you. True power and desire come from a connection with your gut and your cock, not your head.

Get Out of Your Head

Coming into presence starts with getting out of your head. We don't think it is an exaggeration to say that most people spend about 99% of their waking moments in their head. Much of this consists of processing experiences from your past, telling yourself what you should or shouldn't be doing, evaluating and criticizing your own and other's words or actions, and planning the future.

The problem with living your whole life in and from

your head is that knowing what you want or connecting with another person does not come from disembodied heads. If you spend your entire life in your head planning and worrying about the future or reliving or regretting the past, then you don't get the chance to know who you *really* are and what you *really* want. You also don't get to experience the deeper connections that are possible from sex and relationships.

Another option is to live an embodied life where you are present in the moment. Living an embodied life means being connected to your senses and your emotions in the present moment. When you tune into each of your senses and feel what is happening in your body, you appreciate the fullness and satisfaction of every experience you have. Living in your body also means being aware of and making space for your emotions. While, for some, emotions feel extraneous, emotions are biologically essential for people's survival. As social animals, humans need emotions to know what we need and communicate those needs with others. When you allow emotions to move through you instead of trying to stop them or figure them out they flow smoothly and dissolve, leaving you with a sense of lightness and freedom.

Get in Touch with Your Desire

Coming into presence requires that you connect with your sexual body and your sexual desire. These are the parts of your body and psyche that most of your social lessons tell you to distance from and deny. If you really want to know what you want – and get it – you must re-integrate your sexual self into every part of your life.

Picture an animal that is about to mate standing before the object of his desires. He is not planning or worrying about the last time she flew away. He is fully in his own body, connected unequivocally with his sexual arousal in the present moment. He feels every breath, every twitch, every subtle signal of his potential mate. As he reads these signals, he begins a dance that eventually brings him to his goal. If he splits his attention away from this desire or loses connection with the recipient of his desire, he misses the opportunity before him. Staying fully present and attuned to his erotic desire creates his only opportunity for success.

Your power, your confidence and your sexual interactions with women depend on you being in the moment in your erotic body (and eventually reading a woman's queues and responding to them in the moment with your body, not your head). In contrast, planning ahead or trying to come up with the perfect words is an oblivious, detached place to be. This state of detachment is part of what women mean when they say men are "emotionally unavailable." When you are in your head, you are distanced from your own sensation and connection with yourself and from potential moments of erotic energy exchange. When you are in your body, you can feel desire coursing through you and you can generate and read desire in women.

Feel Your Erotic Power

When you are in your body you reconnect with your erotic power - a power that has always been inside you but may have slowly been buried deeper and deeper throughout your life. As men, you get so many conflicting messages about sex. You are told that you are supposed to want sex all the time from anyone and that you are less than a man if you do not try to get it anytime and anywhere you can. You are also told that women don't want sex, that you have to be polite and respectful and shut off your erotic power because it might be harmful to the women around you. What you are not taught is how to engage fully and consciously with your erotic power so you can know what you want and get it while giving women exactly what they want as well.

Pump Up Your Power

One way to feel more masculine power comes from feeling the actual strength that you have in your muscles. This can be achieved quite literally through physical exercise, but it is important to do exercise that supports your sense of masculinity and intensity.

We have noticed that men feel the greatest sense of

transformation and confidence when they begin activities that push them to their physical limits, like weight training or martial arts. Of course, if you are going to begin any exercise program, especially one that is going to push your body to its limits, it is absolutely essential to have the guidance of a professional. Plan on taking a few sessions with a personal trainer to get started.

Find a place to work out that is about serious, powerful exercise and find a trainer or teacher who is willing to take you to your limits while making sure you don't get injured. One of the most important elements to practice when doing these kinds of workouts is using your voice. When you work out hard, you have to breathe, grunt, shout, and sweat. See how present you can be in these moments, focusing completely on the sensation in your body and the pleasure of feeling this kind of power.

Dance is another kind of powerful, confidence-building exercise. Dance is one of the most ancient forms of self-expression and can bring you to a place that is both erotically charged and powerful. It also requires a kind of letting go of physical control of your body and giving yourself a chance to find your body's own natural, creative self-expression. We also strongly encourage you to take some partner dancing classes, especially if you have a difficult time approaching women. Partner dancing classes require you to rotate partners, meet and have physical contact with many different women and, eventually, ask women to dance with you. It is a great way to practice with physical connection and overcome your fear of rejection.

Sex, at the most basic level, is an act of physical connection, creation and creativity. Anything that takes you out of your normal, habitual daily behaviors, requires you to make physical connections and increases your creativity creates new pathways between your brain and your body that can then be strengthened and expanded upon. You may also feel this way after any activity that takes you out of your logical brain and brings you to your body and your creative force.

EXERCISE
The Three Steps to Erotically Embodied Breath

The first exercises in this book are breath-related. You might be thinking, "What does all this breathing have to do with having great sex?" There is a good deal of scientific evidence showing that full, deep relaxed breathing helps the body function from a place of calm presence and awareness. Short, fast breath, on the other hand, tells the body something is amiss; it says you are in a stressed and threatened state and it is time to run or fight, which is no place to be if you want to have great sex.

Connecting intimately and sexually with women is

something you can only do when you are in touch with your body and breath is the first step toward this connection. Think about any body-based activity you have ever done from sports to dance and you will find that consciousness about your breath is essential. Breath is part of martial arts, running, meditation, swimming, and weight training. It is also essential to mastering your sexual function and connecting to your partner during sex. Before connecting with a partner, you must connect with yourself.

When beginning to engage in conscious breath, remember that there is no right way to breathe. When you start these new kinds of breath, you might feel self-conscious at first. Allow yourself to have these feelings. Playing with your breath is about breaking habits and breaking habits always feels a little "weird." Different kinds of breath create different sensations, responses, perceptions, and experiences in your body and mind. Play with different kinds of deep, full breathing throughout your day and experience a greater sense of connection with your body and with the people around you. This connection is an important step towards *Cock-fidence* – which is more than just a connection with your cock; it's a connection with your whole body.

STEP 1 - BASIC BREATH

Basic Breath begins exactly where you are and you can do it right now, wherever you happen to be and in any position. In Basic Breath, you simply come into awareness of your breath and notice how you are breathing. It can be helpful to do this with your eyes closed. It is likely that most of your breath never goes deeper than your chest. If you are highly stressed, it may barely make it below your shoulders.

Begin practicing Basic Breath

- Breathe slowly, gently and deeply in and out through your mouth. Breathing through your mouth encourages the breath more fully and deeply into your body.
- Do not do anything to force the breath.
- Imagine that your stomach, low back, and pelvic floor are relaxing and gently making way for your breath to move more deeply down into your body.
- Take twenty slow, conscious breaths down into your body and simply notice how your body feels.

Answer the following questions:

- What parts of your body are you holding tension in right now that you didn't even realize you were holding until you started breathing?
- Are there places where your body feels relaxed and more open?
- Do you notice any images or memories arise as you breathe more consciously?
- When you open your eyes again after taking these twenty breaths, do you notice anything different about how you see and relate to the world around you?

See what it feels like to try breathing consciously a few times throughout your day and simply notice what happens.

STEP 2 - SEXUAL EMBODIMENT BREATH

To be connected with your sexual self and know what you

want, you must breathe deeply into the parts of your body where desire is generated, namely your gut and your cock. When you first begin practicing this breath, it is best to try it in a private place where you can fully focus your attention on yourself without interruption. Later, the breath becomes a part of who you are so that you can access your desires and your power continuously.

Connecting with your breath in this way brings you more deeply into your desire, intelligence, voice, empathy, power, and passion, while at the same time bringing all of these important aspects of yourself into connection with one another. This is what some people refer to as being "centered" or "grounded."

You can do this breathwork in any position. When first beginning to explore sexual breathing, we have found it easiest to feel the deep movement of the breath and your power by sitting up in a chair or lying on your back. You can experiment with different positions. Visualize that the breath is moving towards different parts of your body - your chest or your stomach for example.

Imagining the breath going towards these parts has the benefit of awakening that part of the body, activating blood flow and creating connections throughout your body. You can imagine the breath coming all the way down into your pelvic floor, connecting you with your cock and all of the power and desire it holds. When you practice breath it is also a practice of being gentle with your body. It is this gentleness that allows your body to begin to relax and feel sexual. Sexual feelings cannot be forced; they can only be invited.

- Sit in a chair with your feet planted on the floor and, as in the Basic Breath, bring consciousness to your breath.
- Notice how deeply you breathe, what parts of your body move when you breathe, whether you hold your breath after the inhale or after the exhale.
- Place your hand in the center of your chest and take ten slow, deep breaths directed into your chest.
  - Do not force your breath but allow your chest to open as the breath flows towards your hand.
  - Feel the breath rise and fall in your upper body and visualize yourself opening to sensations in this part of your body and to your emotional self.
  - Notice if there is any tension in your neck and back and bring the breath to those places, inviting them to come to a deeper level of relaxation.
- Place your hand on your solar plexus, the upper part of your stomach right below your ribcage, and take ten slow, deep breaths into your stomach.
  - Let go of being goal-oriented as you breathe into your solar plexus.
  - Feel the breath rise and fall in your stomach and visualize yourself opening to sensations in this part of your body and to your personal power.
  - Feel your free will and your boundaries. The ability to say "yes" *and* "no" have profound effects on your ability to feel sexual energy in your body.
- Moving down deeper into your body, place your hand on your cock and bring the breath all the way down to your pelvic floor.

- Notice what reflex, if any, happens around your pelvic floor when you breathe deeply directing your breath towards your cock.

- The basis of breathing into your cock is to encourage relaxation in your pelvic floor. As you breathe in simply direct your attention toward your cock and imagine that this area is getting more relaxed.

- On the exhale, the idea is to do nothing but simply allow your body to fully release the breath and let go. By letting go of controlling your breath and muscles, you can feel your body open to eroticism.

- Allow your consciousness to move deeply into your pelvis and genitals. As you engage fully in this breath, you may start to feel some tingling or awakening.

STEP 3 - EROTIC POWER BREATH

Breath that directly addresses erotic power is the basis of *Cockfidence*. This breath connects your throat, chest, stomach and pelvis and is a metaphor for connecting your voice, emotion, power, and sexual energy. We call it Erotic Power Breath. This breath creates a combination of relaxation and arousal in your body; this combination of relaxation and arousal is the perfect place from which to meet women and to have sex with them.

- Begin by breathing in through your mouth and bringing the breath all the way down to your cock, where we finished in the last breathing exercise. Take twenty slow, deep breaths all the way down to your cock.

- On your next inhale, squeeze the muscles in your cock like you are stopping yourself from urinating then exhale and release the breath.

- Take twenty fast breaths with these squeezes.
- Go through three cycles of power breath taking twenty, slow, deep breaths and then twenty fast, squeezing and releasing breaths. You can actually do as many cycles of this power breath as you want, but minimally, to get the full effect in your body, do at least three cycles.
- End your final cycle with The Big Draw.
  - To do The Big Draw, inhale through your nose and exhale through your mouth three times. On the third breath, inhale and hold your breath. *Do not let it out.*
  - As you are holding your breath, squeeze the muscles in your cock, your pelvic floor, your fists, your chest, your legs, your feet your face and hold, hold, hold.
  - Release the breath and feel the rush of erotic power and energy move through your body. It can be very helpful to release with sound, which invites the energy to shoot up through your whole body.

At the end of this breathing experience, take a moment to notice if you feel a difference anywhere in your body.
Answer these questions:

- Do you feel more powerful and open?
- Is there a greater sense of relaxation and aliveness?
- Are you aware of tension you didn't know you had?
- Did any resistance come up?

When you first start practicing with all three of these breaths, you might feel resistant or dizzy. Sometimes this kind of breathing takes time to have its amazingly positive effects. Once you get the hang of it, it will be one way to help you walk through the world with a greater sense of erotic power. Most importantly, it brings you fully into presence with the moment and your erotic energy, turning you into a magnet that women notice and respond to in their own sexual bodies.

Try doing the Sexual Embodiment Breath and the Erotic Power Breath before leaving the house for a date, before a walk out in the world, before a visit to the local coffee shop, and notice the ways that people respond to you differently.

Acceptance

A cceptance means having relationships with others where you celebrate those aspects of the person you enjoy and desire and realizing that there is nothing you can do to change the parts that make you uncomfortable or upset. The way people change is when they are personally inspired for their own reasons to do so. Acceptance is not the same as settling. To accept your partner exactly as she is doesn't mean going along with things that don't work for you. The solution is not to change her but to express your needs and your boundaries. When you can do this with love and acceptance, you give her the safety of discovering herself and what she is capable of. With clear requests and non-defensive boundaries, you can take care of yourself and open doors for her to do the same.

Being a truly *Cockfident* man and an Extraordinary

Lover to women takes a tremendous amount of acceptance of yourself, your partner, and the people who are part of your life. A deep sense of power and freedom comes from acceptance, because acceptance allows you to know, at the most basic level, that everything is okay. This kind of acceptance means relearning how to listen to your emotions, something that boys are trained away from early in life. It means letting go of perfection and finding out what "good enough" means. Finally, it means making space for your partner to be who she is instead of wishing she lived up to your fantasies or desires.

Listen to Your Emotions

Recent research on men has shown that men actually have much stronger immediate emotional reactions than women. Also they successfully quell their emotions and move into thinking, figuring out, and fixing much more quickly than women.

There is a huge difference between men's and women's culture in our upbringing. We were at the playground one warm, summer day and two little boys were fighting. One of the boys hit the other and he sat down and began to cry. His father stood above him, did not touch him and said, "Don't cry - if you don't want him to hit you, you need to show him that you are tough and hit him back." The little boy tried to pull himself together. Still crying he punched the other boy in the shoulder.

The fight escalated to the point where one of the moms noticed and pulled them apart, but not before both children got the clear message that being a man means being tough and hiding your emotions.

The lack of freedom that men have in regard to acknowledging and listening to their emotions leads men to think that they are making rational decisions, when they are often unconsciously making emotional decisions or making decisions that discount their emotional needs completely.

When you ignore your emotions they are relegated to the unconscious; when you are unconscious your emotions can control your behaviors without you having any understanding of what is driving you. On the other hand, if you discount your emotional needs in service of making rational decisions, you end up living a life that seems "right" but doesn't *feel* good.

You might fear feeling your emotions because you fear they seem unmanly, irrational, and dependent, while everything in this culture gives you the message that you are always supposed to appear strong, reasonable, and self-sufficient. While it might feel safer to distance from your emotions, emotions are actually at the foundation of power, intimacy and passion. You cannot be an Extraordinary Lover without being in touch with your emotions and being able to express them – shutting these emotions means shutting off your body – your greatest tool in being a lover. The *Cockfident* man is not the man standing alone on a hill with a bulletproof chest, hands on his hips, impervious to the world's troubles. He is a man that can experience his emotions with his friends and lovers.

Unexpressed and unprocessed emotions, like anger and sadness, tie up your sexual energy and block your erotic power. If left unexplored, these emotions can block you from experiencing the height of your sexual expression. What's more, unexpressed emotions are often the root of sexual difficulties such as the inability to get an erection or the inability to ejaculate with a partner. In order to regain access to your powerful erotic energy, you have to shine some light on your emotional self.

In their purest form, anger and sadness are positive emotions with essential information about how you want to live your life. People think of sadness and anger as negative emotions because they make us feel uncomfortable, but it is this discomfort that is emotion's greatest gift. The discomfort of anger or sadness says something needs to change. When men avoid these so-called "negative" emotions, the emotions build up and transform into rage, resentment, depression, and resignation, leaving men feeling stuck and hopeless.

Sometimes if you have been living with these secondary emotions for a while, they begin to feel like home. In fact, they can develop as a way to protect yourself, forming a safety zone that you can use to keep from connecting with others. In order to experience power and intimacy, you must move through these stuck emotions, back to anger or sadness. Delving into these emotions unleashes your confined energy, transforming it into motivation, power, attraction, passion and creativity.

In addition to the freedom you gain when you let yourself feel and move through anger or sadness, both of these emotions can also be powerful teachers about how you relate to women. Anger and sadness let you know your boundaries and help you cope with the inherent difficulties that are part of life. When you allow them, it is possible for them to arise, be felt and flow through.

If you find that anger or sadness are coming up over and over again around the same topics and across multiple relationships, the first step is to identify them so you can let yourself feel them. It is essential to explore these emotions and ask yourself, "What part of this is an old wound that has very little to do with what is going on between my partner and me right now?" When you begin to do this, you will find that there are more effective, healthy and transformative ways of dealing with your emotions.

The trick to identifying your emotions is to pay attention to what you feel in your body. When anger or sadness well up you will find that you have your own individual sensation that goes along with those emotions.

Anger commonly feels like an adrenaline rush combined with a tightness most often felt in the chest, stomach, throat and/or shoulders. Sadness is commonly a heavy feeling combined with the feeling that there is a painful, empty space like a hole in your body, most often in the chest or solar plexus.

When one of these feelings wells up, most often you talk yourself out of it, push it back down, try to make it go away or lash out. Usually because there is adrenaline in the body or a desire to change this feeling quickly, you take immediate action. Instead take a moment and say, "There is no urgency here, I have time to see how I am feeling before deciding what to do." Just as when there is a fire and they tell you to "Stop, Drop and Roll," when you feel the fire of emotion inside of you, try "Stop, Breathe, and Listen." You can break the habitual response to anger or sadness by simply not doing whatever you usually do and listening instead. Listen to your body, your emotions, and the kinds of feedback you are getting. Just listen. Slowly, over time, you begin to gain enough skill in these moments to do some deeper searching.

Try the following seven steps to get more deeply in touch with your emotions:

1. **Sensation** – Stop trying to figure out your feelings and start to feel them. This means letting go of your thoughts and noticing the sensations in your

body. Notice the qualities or imagery of the sensation (i.e., pressure in your chest, a brick wall between your stomach and pelvis, a tightness in your throat, shakiness in your hands, etc.).

2. **History** – Track these sensations back to their source. Ask yourself what the sensation is and what just happened that led your body to feel this way. Is this an old feeling, have I felt it before? What kinds of experiences in my life have led me to feel this way? How do I usually respond? Do I go on the attack? Do I retreat? Do I freeze up? How does this response generally turn out? What old fears are underlying this anger/sadness or what fears am I avoiding?

3. **Curiosity** – Take a non-judgmental approach to learning about what is making you angry or sad in this moment. It is rarely what you think. Usually, it has to do with a feeling that some core part of your identity or a belief is being attacked or misunderstood (i.e., she is saying I'm not a good man, good partner or good lover) or that there is some underlying fear (i.e., I am not lovable, worthy or needed).

4. **Gentleness** – What kinds of messages am I giving myself when I feel this way? Am I beating myself up? How am I treating others when I feel this way? Can I be gentle with both myself and others

through this process?

5. **Reality Check** – Come into the present moment. Become a compassionate witness to your experience and emotions. Ask yourself, "What is actually going on here? Are all the fears that are coming up really present in this moment or are they old beliefs and feelings that I have held for a long time?"

6. **Responsibility** – Feeling powerful in your personal relationships is about taking responsibility. You might be angry at someone that you feel has hurt you or done you wrong, however, you can't change someone else, but you can change your habitual response. Ask yourself, "What new stories and ways of responding can I embrace so that I am in alignment with who I am now?" and "What do I really want out of this interaction?"

7. **Communication** – Share with the person how you felt without expecting them to do what you want them to do. You will have a much easier time expressing how you feel and what you need in a way that leads to getting closer to those you care about rather than pushing them away. When communicating start your sentences with "I feel" and then share an emotion. If there is something that you want to say to your partner about what is going on in your relationship, talk about what you feel in response to what she did. Describe what she did neu-

trally instead of accusatorily. For example, "When you told me that the way I talked to our son was ridiculous, I felt hurt and criticized." (For more about this way of communicating, look at websites about Non-Violent Communication such as http://www.cnvc.org/).

Face Your Fear of Rejection

One of the most difficult things about being a man in this culture is that men are largely responsible for approaching women, initiating contact and escalating sexual experiences. This is very vulnerable and risky because it opens you up to the possibility that your desires may not be received and reciprocated. Facing your fear of rejection is one of the most powerful steps a man can take. The truth is, not every woman is going to want what you have to offer in the moment that you offer it (yes, this means she might want it later so it is important to not give up right away). Fear of rejection limits your desire to approach a woman or to fully open yourself to her. By staying closed and avoiding connection, you attempt to avoid rejection. Any rejection can trigger core fears (and mistaken beliefs) such as "Something is wrong with me" or "I am unlovable."

Men deal with the fear of rejection in two major ways. One way is to maintain an objectifying relationship to women, connecting through physical satisfaction alone.

They focus all of their attention on getting sex because they have lost trust in the possibility of real connection. They attempt to make the woman smaller than she is by avoiding her deeper qualities, and people often refer to these men as "users" or "players."

There are also men who fear rejection so much that they see woman as much bigger or more powerful than themselves. They feel women are unreachable or constantly judging them. They are often unable to see the moments when a woman opens up to them and they are constantly waiting for permission and depending on her assurance that they are wanted before they even let themselves feel their desires, let alone act on them. This is how men end up in the "nice guy" or "friend" category. Neither of these approaches results in real connection.

Dealing with feelings of rejection is not easy. It requires a very important shift in the way you feel - namely separating your desire from its outcome. So many of us define success by what we get instead of the bravery of trying to get it. To allow yourself to want what you want and go for it is the true success and deserves a tremendous amount of celebration. If you get what you tried for that's wonderful, if you don't, take the time to allow yourself to feel your disappointment and your desire that it be different. Getting what you want does not define success, knowing you truly tried and that you were brave enough to ask, that is the moment when you are saying to yourself and your spirit, "My desires are important enough to go after" and "I am worth it." When you are a *Cockfident* man you make yourself vulnerable to rejection because you put your true self out there. Yet, you are also accepting of yourself in every moment whether you are getting a "yes" or a "no" – this acceptance allows you to know your desires and continue to pursue them no matter what.

Let Go of Perfection

Since no one is ever perfect, perfectionism is the biggest enemy of acceptance. Often when you expect yourself to be perfect, you also have unreasonably high expectations of a partner, which inevitably leads to huge disappointments.

The desire to be perfect usually comes from having highly critical or conditional parents. You internalize the critical voice and it sticks around. Many people use criticism and striving for perfection as a way to avoid rejection and mistakes. In reality, it is actually the fear of making a mistake that hinders you from moving forward in your life in many ways. While people feel that trying to be perfect inspires them to change, the truth is it generally leaves people paralyzed, fearing making any move because it might be a mistake. This has negative consequences in every area of your life, and especially in your connections with women. True inspiration, motivation and change come from having a deep acceptance of who you are.

Of course you are going to make mistakes. Of course you didn't and don't do everything perfectly. You can give yourself the acceptance that you probably didn't get when you were younger. When you find acceptance for yourself, you regain excitement about life and a passionate desire to live life fully.

In your present life, you can realize that you don't need to beat yourself up anymore. You can be the one to tell yourself you are okay, attractive and worthy. Unlike criticism and self-hatred, acceptance is actually a huge catalyst for change. When you have acceptance and compassion for yourself and the people around you, change happens so much more easily. When you accept yourself as perfectly imperfect, you have room inside of your body to receive love and connection.

Because no one is 100% what another person wants, when you open yourself to a woman, you also open yourself to potentially hearing that you are not what she really needs in the moment, that she doesn't trust you, or that you are not doing it right. When you feel a sense of self-acceptance, you feel more comfortable and grounded in the face of her criticisms. Then you will be able to open yourself up and be vulnerable in relationships because you won't believe or buy into the idea that her distress means something is wrong with you. You know that you are okay.

To gain a deeper sense of self-acceptance, we invite you to:

- **Throw your critical voice out the window.** This may seem simple but it is not easy. If you have encountered a lot of criticism in your life, you will have a very strong internalized critical voice. This voice, however is not *you* and you don't deserve to be talked to that way by anyone, let alone yourself.

- **Any time your critical voice comes in say something that counters it.** If your critical voice says, "Well, you really fucked up again this time," try saying, "You really did the very best you could this time." If your critical voice continues to run your life, you may need to get some help and support in learning ways to deal with this voice, it's a tough one.

- **Celebrate your day-to-day accomplishments.** There will never be a time when everything is perfect. Instead of waiting, find little victories to celebrate every day.

One final note on letting go of perfection: many people think that there is some part of themselves that they have to get rid of before they can really connect with someone and be accepted for who they are. The truth is that we all have many parts of ourselves and they are all here to stay. When you can accept all of your parts and love yourself unconditionally, including all of the parts you believe are flawed, then you can let go of the pressure of pushing those parts away whenever they arise. These previously hated or shunned parts move into a gentle balance with all of your other qualities.

Accept, Don't Compromise

Common wisdom tells us that relationships require compromise. For the most part, we disagree. We see most of the compromises people make in relationships as more of a slippery slope to losing who you really are than the necessary step to a lasting relationship.

It is one thing to learn to put the toilet seat down because it bothers your sweetie and an entirely different thing to decide that you or your partner has to put an essential part of yourself away in order to maintain a relationship. One example is a client of ours who likes to be playful, tickle and joke around with his wife. She complains that this is childish so he stops, but he feels more and more disconnected from her because this is one his favorite ways to initiate connection. Instead of trying to understand what her underlying feelings were or respecting his own needs, he just compromised and lost an important part of himself. The urge to compromise came from the desire to fix her discomfort and solve the problem. A longer conversation with her revealed that when he tickled and joked around, she felt like he was treating her like a friend and that he didn't really desire her sexually. Once he learned how to seduce her from a *Cockfident* place and she felt his passion, she was also able to enjoy his playfulness as well.

The craziest thing about compromising is that people often make compromises based upon assumptions without ever verifying whether these assumptions are true or not. This happens all the time in regard to sex. For example, you say to yourself, "I'm sure my partner would never want to do _____ sexually so I'll just try to make myself not want it." The problem is, when it comes to our deepest desires, it is impossible to make yourself not want them so you begin blaming your partner for keeping you from what you want. Sometimes people find those things elsewhere secretly, other times they shut down out of resentment or lose track of their own path.

Instead of compromising who you are, try sharing with, listening to and accepting the multiplicity of desires and parts of yourself *and* your partner. Unlike compromise, true freedom requires honest communication and internal work to go through all of the feelings that come up when you or your partner want something that feels threatening or uncomfortable to the other person.

One of the main feelings you may be trying to avoid in compromising instead of working on acceptance is your or your partner's disappointment. When you actually acknowledge that you cannot be everything to your partner and she cannot be everything to you then you can both allow yourselves to feel the disappointment, share it with each other and come up with creative ways to meet your needs or let them go. Communicating with your partner about your needs allows you to find out what you can and can't meet for one another and what you are both comfortable with getting elsewhere in life. The payoff for this communication and work is immense because it can lead to truly, deeply and uncompromisingly satisfying relationships.

EXERCISE
Tracking Your Own Emotions

In the coming week, begin to pay attention and track your emotions. Many times, you may not even realize that you are having an emotion, however, you might feel a difference in your mood and the sensations in your body. For example, you are in a work meeting, and your boss criticizes your new project plan. You ignore the tightness in your chest, and the rush of blood to your face and, instead, you begin solving the problem. Solving the problem from this place of tightness, however, usually ends in frustration and creative blocks.

Instead, try this. Wait for the meeting to be over, go back to your desk and take a minute to notice and feel the sensations in your body. Allow yourself to feel the tightness and acknowledge whatever is there. It may be defensiveness, anger, rejection, frustration or anxiety. Just by noticing and allowing the emotions, your body may relax and loosen a bit and allow you to reconnect with all of your creative resources. Use your body throughout the week to track all of the responses you are having. This helps you know what you are feeling and have more compassion for yourself. Cultivating this kind of compassion is also essential to having empathy for others (For more on Empathy, see Quality 6)

It is also important to name your emotions. We have included a list of the most commonly used emotion words for you to look at in order to increase your emotional vocabulary. This helps you to communicate your emotions when you feel ready to do so. You can find more comprehensive lists online.

Emotion	Opposite Emotion
Afraid	Safe
Sad	Happy
Rejected	Desired
Ignored	Heard
Invisible	Seen
Taken for Granted	Appreciated
Lonely/Alone	Connected
Ashamed	Proud
Bored	Excited

Confused	Clear
Misunderstood	Understood
Insecure	Confident

Other common emotions that you might feel include: angry, supported, hurt, relaxed, pushed, accepted, confused, jealous, loved, frustrated, resentful, and acknowledged.

Confidence

onfidence is the state of knowing that you have a right to your desires and the ability to pursue them, combined with the self-assurance that women want you and you can satisfy them both relationally and sexually. It is the sentence, "I know who I am and what I want, and I know that I've got what you want."

Having this kind of confidence gives you an embodied feeling of personal power; nothing feels better than being fully confident about who you are and what you want. Women are extremely attracted to confident men. Many men, especially those who have fallen into the "nice guy" category, complain that women date jerks. They think that if they could just start treating women badly, they would get a lot more dates. The reason that women are willing to put up with men who treat them badly is that these men often also project false confidence and are willing to approach them and "take them" sexually. Women don't really want jerks – they trade getting treated badly for having hot sex. As you gain *Cockfidence* and become an Extraordinary Lover, you can provide what they want without being a jerk!

Unfortunately for women, the reason that so-called jerks seem to have confidence is that they are in a distanced, protected and objectified relationship with women and are unconsciously attempting not to care about women. While it may seem so much easier to be confident when you don't actually care about the person that you are approaching, you also don't get the benefits of connected sex. The benefits of connected sex include higher states of sexual arousal due to a full exchange of erotic energy, a greater sense of self-worth that comes from mutual respect and integrity, a higher chance of open communication and reciprocity so you are more likely to get what you want sexually and to satisfy your partner.

When you care about the women that you are fucking (which does not necessarily mean that you are in a relationship or exclusive with them, just that you care), you can experience all of the benefits of connected sex and have the kind of confidence that women really want. In the same way that you want a woman who is both caring and sexually open, women want it all as well – they want a man who deeply cares about and desires them and who brings the kind of confidence that helps them connect with their own power and sexuality.

It is unfortunate how much women are willing to put up with to be with a seemingly confident man who is willing to go after what he wants and take charge in bed. Ultimately, however, women do not want to be treated poorly, which is why, in our workshops, we always say, "Women want nice guys who fuck like jerks." The truth is, women do want you to care about them, and, at the same time, they respond sexually to someone who is confident in his own life and in sexual situations.

There are external signals of confidence that many so-called dating experts teach men to mimic outwardly in order to trick women into thinking they are confident. This is a short-term fix and not a long-term solution. An erect posture and eye contact may help pique her interest, but, if you do not feel confidence fully and deeply in your body, a woman can tell and she is far less likely to put her desire and her sexuality into your hands. If you have ever felt the moment when a woman realized you were faking confidence, you know it can be devastating. In order to find your own embodied sense of confidence, that is authentic to you, you must get in touch with your own sense of self.

Most men feel confident around women when they feel like they possess what a woman wants or when they can satisfy her desires. While it feels wonderful to have positive messages from your partner about how fantastic you are in bed or in the way that you relate to her, you cannot depend on your partner to give you this feeling. Your feeling of confidence must come from inside of yourself.

When you feel confidence in your body, you walk through the world with certainty in your step, your shoulders are back and your chest is open, your hands swing loosely at your side instead of hiding inside your pockets, your head is up and women around you are reacting to you with their bodies. They turn their heads to look at you, they smile as you walk by, their hands move to their hair, primping when they see you coming. All of this confidence in your body and the reactions from outside create a self-perpetuating cycle. This kind of embodied confidence is not an act; it's a physical expression of what you feel inside.

You know you have found embodied confidence when you feel:

- **Grounded** - you can feel your feet on the ground and the power in your legs.
- **Centered** - you feel an open channel running from your cock to your head.
- **Relaxed** - you lack tension in your shoulders, chest, stomach, back, butt and legs.
- **Aroused** - your body feels awake and alive, energy

is flowing, and you are aware of sensation in your cock.

When you are in your body in this way with a woman, you find yourself in amazing, fluid conversations. She laughs with you and listens in rapt attention to everything you are saying. Your questions bring her to her deepest interests, desires and passions. You don't even have to think about what you are going to say next, everything just flows.

Connect with Other Men

It may be surprising, but a part of feeling really confident and powerful in the world is about having other men you feel connected to - men who support you and who challenge you to be the best person you can be. We live in a society that makes men's ability to connect with one another quite difficult. Boys learn early on that any kind of physical closeness with another boy is punishable by homophobic epithets such as "fag" and "homo." If a boy is labeled a sissy or shows any kind of weakness that might indicate vulnerability, he usually becomes the victim of violence or other kinds of painful bullying.

Competition can be a very positive aspect of growing up - it helps boys feel their own strength and learn how to work together. In fact, one way that men support each other is by helping each other "toughen up." On the other hand, intense, pressured competition can also make boys fearful to ever show any kind of weakness to another boy. This leaves men feeling that they cannot be vulnerable with anyone, and especially not with other men.

The problem with keeping your distance from other men is that you sacrifice the support from close, male friends. Connecting with men, on the other hand, fosters a feeling of belonging and camaraderie. When there are men out there who have your back and your best interest at heart, you feel less dependent on approval from women and more powerful in your life.

When men avoid other men, it is often because they don't trust masculine power. The truth is, there are many men out there who abuse their male power. They hurt women, they hurt each other and they hurt themselves. Just because these kinds of men exist in the world does not mean that masculine power is inherently abusive or hurtful. It means there is a calling for men who can fully experience their masculine power and do right by women and towards other men and themselves. When you embody this kind of masculinity, you not only feel your own full sense of power, you also become the invitation to other men to behave in this way.

Try taking small steps to be vulnerable with the men in your life. Take conversations to a deeper level by talking about your desires and struggles in life, work and relationships. These conversations with other men can help you rediscover and reclaim a part of yourself that may have been missing for a long time. In addition to communication, physical touch from other men in the form of hugs or a hand on the shoulder can also connect you with a deep, missing, compassionate piece of yourself. Connecting with other men in these ways is a big part of confidence because you go out in the world with the sense that other men are not your enemies, but your allies.

When you have a male friend or a group of male friends who you can really trust with this vulnerability, and who call you on your shit, you find a deeper sense of compassion for yourself. When you feel compassion from other men, you can bring this compassion to women. When your male friends have your back, you feel more powerful in all your interactions with women.

Do Not Put Yourself Above or Below Others

Happiness experts tell you that comparing yourself to others and deciding that you have come up short is one of the swiftest ways to depression and loneliness. At the same time, feeling confident has nothing to do with feeling better than other people. Quite the contrary, when you feel confident, you are happy when everyone else around you is succeeding and happy as well. You support them and they support you.

Looking to others who you respect for inspiration is

a great motivator. It is only when you begin to imagine that you are behind them in some race that you forget your unique gifts and passions and you lose confidence, self-respect and your own path. Also, putting everyone else down or comparing yourself to those you feel are inferior to pump up your ego is the easiest way to end up self-centered and lonely. On the other hand, celebrating others' accomplishments with them creates deeper connections and is very nourishing to yourself as well.

When you really listen in to your own passions, strengths and gifts, and stop comparing yourself to others to decide whether you are a success or failure, you find the confidence that fills your body with power and is so attractive to women.

Realize Your Sexual Potential

To feel the full force of your confidence, you must be sure that you are at the height of your sexual potential and the master of your sexual function. While almost every man is capable of achieving an orgasm, as you may already know, your orgasms can range from "Okay" to "OH MY GOD." The surest way to attain the height of your sexual potential is to become the master of your sexual function. You can feel the full force of your sexual desire, experience powerful erections, come when you are ready and experience the power and pleasure of full-body sensation and orgasms. You have the ability to feel the heights and depths of your sexual potential, and the process of getting there can be fun and pleasurable. What's more, women are highly responsive to men's sexual desire and pleasure.

Master Your Sexual Function

The confidence that comes from mastering your sexual function does not come from always being able to perform exactly how you want all the time - this is an impossible goal. A sense of mastery comes when you learn everything you can about how your body works sexually, experience your full sexual potential, accept that your performance can have ups and downs, and be able to communicate with your partner about it.

Whether or not you have ever experienced challenges to your sexual function, every man should read this section. If there is one guarantee that comes with having a body, it's that your body changes throughout your lifetime and it won't always do what you want it to do. At some point in their lives, men experience ejaculating when they don't want to, not being hard when they want to, etc. It is important to give your cock the message that he doesn't always have to be hard and last forever. Your connections with women, whether they are long-term, new or casual, can survive sexual ups and downs!

Read this section to help you catch early signs of sexual problems and turn the tide before your body becomes habituated to any negative patterns. No matter where you currently are in terms of your body's capacity, we have found that pleasure-based approaches are the best way to attain mastery.

Because of our culture's obsession with orgasm and intercourse, many men and women believe that men having full control of their sexual function will suddenly fix their sex life. This is based on the assumption that what women really need to get off is for a man to stay hard long enough and then come right on target. While it is wonderful for your confidence and your own pleasure to have mastery over your sexual function, there is so much more to sex than just intercourse. In fact, intercourse is not the be-all end-all of sex for women, and many women do not come through intercourse at all. We will explain all about women's orgasms in the second section.

There is so much pressure, shame and silence around sexual performance for men that many men suffer needlessly for years with sexual challenges that could easily be resolved. The most common desire around mastery for men is to gain control over the timing of their ejaculation so that they can last longer. The lack of this ability is commonly referred to as early ejaculation or premature ejaculation. The next most common desire is to be able to get an erection with a partner whenever they are ready for one. The lack of this ability is commonly referred to as erectile dysfunction.

We do not refer to these as sexual dysfunctions. This is because many instances of what doctors and sex therapists refer to as a sexual dysfunction is actually a *functional response to a dysfunctional situation or belief.* In other words, quick ejaculation, inability to get an erection or an inability to orgasm may be your body giving you an important message. It may be saying, "This situation is too anxiety producing for me and I am not comfortable." Or, it may be saying, "When she is critical of me all the time, I don't really want to go inside her" or "I don't know how to trust a woman enough to fully let go with her," or "I'm going to get in and out really quickly because she probably doesn't like this."

Some sexual difficulties do have a medical origin and it is a good idea to get tested. One way to evaluate whether or not you should get tested is by looking at whether the sexual issue or issues you want to work on are situational or come up in every sexual situation, whether it be masturbation or partnered sex. In other words, if you are having difficulties getting an erection when you are with a particular partner but have no problem at all when you are masturbating, this is a situational problem and is probably more in your head than in your body. If, on the other hand, you used to have strong erections whether masturbating or with a partner and you have recently started having much weaker erections in all of your sexual and masturbatory experiences, you should get checked out by a doctor or medical professional.

Talk to Your Partner

Unfortunately, women often take your experiences with performance difficulties very personally. If you can't get an erection, they think they don't turn you on. If you come quickly, a woman might feel like you are just using her for your pleasure and aren't willing to take the time to make her feel good. Most of the time, however, this is not the case at all. When you communicate openly about sexual challenges you have from a calm place of confidence in your sexuality, it is much harder for women to take them so personally. The most important thing you can do in the face of erectile challenges is to reassure her that she does turn you on, but sometimes your erection is there and other times it is not. If your partner does not turn you on, that's an example of a functional response to a dysfunctional situation and you need to look at why you are choosing to have sex with her.

While continuing to take time to work on your sexual function and pleasure, also discuss how the two of you can broaden the focus of your sex life together so that intercourse is not the only act in your repertoire. This expansion might include manual and oral stimulation, toys, talking dirty, mutual masturbation, sharing fantasies, etc.

Let Go of Performance

If we take a broad-brush approach to the idea of sexual mastery, we can say that blocks to mastery are, in almost every case, perpetuated and exacerbated by anxiety about performance. It is not surprising that a lot of men experience performance anxiety since boys are socialized around having to prove they are always capable and competent. When men doubt their competence they begin to lose confidence in themselves, which leads to performance anxiety.

Often, long before intercourse even begins, at the first thought that it might be time to have sex, men become anxious and worried that they will not be able to get hard or time their ejaculation. This anxiety constricts the blood vessels and keeps men in their minds and disconnected from their bodies, making it much more likely for sexual challenges to arise.

You can take pressure off your cock by understanding what women really want from sex and learning how to fuck a woman's brains out before you even take your pants off. To put it simply (though it is complex and we'll break it down for you later) what women really want from sex is an emotional experience. Women have sex to *feel* something! It doesn't necessarily have to be love or commitment, but something. They want to feel your desire (for your own pleasure and for them) and they want to feel you are fully present. If you ejaculate quickly and then feel guilty or ashamed you will likely distance from your partner and she may feel left alone or abandoned.

Instead, if you really make her feel something and give her and her body all the attention it needs, she will be lying there a puddle of post orgasmic bliss, with little concern if sometimes you last longer and sometimes it goes quickly. This way, you can take the pressure off of your cock as you continue to pursue better mastery.

To pursue better mastery, you can directly confront the cycle of anxiety with a few simple steps:

+ **Notice sensation in your body.** Where is it feeling tight? Where is it feeling relaxed? Can you feel your arms and legs? Is there tightness in your chest or stomach?

+ **Breathe.** Practice your Sexual Embodiment Breath and allow your body to unclench. Breathe directly into any parts that feel tight and imagine them releasing and relaxing with the breath.

+ **Relax your mind.** One way to do this is by giving yourself calming messages that help you unclench your body and let go of destructive and anxiety perpetuating thoughts. Instead of paying attention to what might be wrong, notice what is happening in your body with curiosity, not judgment. Try giving yourself positive messages around your body and pleasure like, "My body can give and receive pleasure just as it is" and "It feels good to touch and be touched."

+ **Connect with pleasurable sensation.** Often,

when you begin struggling with sexual issues, you lose connection with the extraordinary pleasure sex can (and possibly once did) offer you. Continue breathing deeply and using the breath to connect you with any sensations in your body that feel arousing, erotic, sensual or pleasurable. Bring your mind into connection with your body by saying, "I can feel pleasure in my _____ (fill in the blank, i.e., hands, stomach)." Continue to relax and connect with that sensation. Focusing back toward pleasure can really help turn the tides of performance anxiety.

Control Your Ejaculation

To control your ejaculation, begin with the Letting Go of Performance exercises. Next, you need to slow down and gather some information about what is going on in your body. You also need to learn or remember how to enjoy pleasure in your body and how to hold and build sexual intensity.

Slow Down

Before you do anything else slow down, *way down*. Men who have issues with ejaculation control are usually in a hurry in every part of their life. They often approach life with a desire to do everything quickly and easily. They sit down in front of us and say, "So, how long is this going to take? What kind of measurable results can I hope for and when? I tried a bunch of different things but nothing worked." If you are in a hurry in most areas of your life, it is not surprising that you come quickly.

You may also be somewhat of an overachiever; you may look at sex and other kinds of pleasure as a luxury that you can't afford to spend too much time on since there are so many other things you need to get done in your life. Sexual fulfillment, however, is a very important pursuit; it makes you happier, more efficient, more productive, more successful and more attractive to other successful people.

Gather Information

The first homework we always give men is to masturbate. Most of them laugh and say, "Well, that's easy." Aside from being a fun, easy homework assignment, this first masturbation session allows you to tune into what is happening in your body. During your masturbation session, we want you to pay attention to five things:

1. **Breath** – How are you breathing, and particularly how do you breathe right before you orgasm and during orgasm? Do you breathe through your mouth or nose, do you breathe quickly or slowly, do you hold your breath at any point?

2. **Muscles** – What do you do with your muscles? At any point during masturbation, do you squeeze the

muscles in your legs, face or throat?

3. **Touch** – What parts of your body do you touch, what kinds of strokes do you use on your cock? Do you touch any other parts of your body (i.e., your balls, your nipples, your stomach, etc.)

4. **Arousal Pattern** – What is your arousal pattern? Is it a slow building of sexual energy followed by a deep, full release or is it a sudden spike followed by immediate orgasm/ejaculation? Does it move up and down during the course of your masturbation or is it only getting higher?

5. **Point of No Return** – The point of no return, also called ejaculatory inevitability, is that feeling you have when you know you are going to come and there is nothing you can do about it. Pay attention to what the point of no return feels like. Where do you feel it (i.e., in your cock, in your balls, in your perineum, in your asshole)? What does it feel like right before the point of no return?

Answering these questions helps you get in touch with what is actually going on in your body. Then you can follow these physiological approaches towards ejaculatory mastery.

Spread the Pleasure

Let go of the idea that the goal is orgasm and focus on the enjoyment of the sensation of pleasure. In general, men's sexuality is much more genitally and orgasmically focused than women's. When you learn to spread your sexual energy through your body, your sexuality actually becomes much more powerful and compatible with women's sexuality.

Your entire body becomes a sex organ and, once you orgasm (with or without ejaculation), you feel the orgasm shoot through your whole body. This is called a full-body orgasm. If you have not yet experienced a full-body orgasm, you are in for a treat. If you are ejaculating really quickly, the chances of you having a full body orgasm are slim since a full-body orgasm requires that a certain level of sexual intensity be built up inside of your body before you can feel it shooting up through your head and out through your toes.

Stay with Your Own Sensations

Another important skill is to stay in touch with sensation in your own body. Men who have a difficult time controlling their ejaculation are often overly pre-occupied with giving women pleasure and focus so much on being concerned about their partner's pleasure they lose touch with the sensations and processes that are taking place in their own bodies. Don't get us wrong; we believe that men should want to give women pleasure, so listen closely. First of all, the best way to intuitively know what is making a woman feel pleasure is by connecting the feelings and sensations in your own body with the feelings and sensations in your partner's body. Second, it is essential to remember that women get a tremendous amount of pleasure by knowing that you are feeling pleasure. When you are in your body and focused on your pleasure, your arousal positively affects hers and you continue to build together.

Conventional wisdom teaches men that controlling ejaculation means distancing from pleasure in the body by thinking of things that are boring, anti-sexual or downright disgusting. We've heard men trying everything from baseball statistics to their grandmother. We even had a client who said he used to joke with his girlfriend that he was "Mick Jaggering," by which he meant that he would think of Mick Jagger in order to try to get himself to last longer. While this might work in the short run, the more likely outcome is that he has a rapid ejaculation every time he sees a Stones video.

Research shows that distancing is not the best approach to mastering your ejaculation. Instead, really sensing into the body and its responses helps men have better control over their ejaculation.

Breathe

As always, you have to breathe. We have found that Sexual Embodiment Breath focused towards the asshole is the most effective type of breath for ejaculation control, partly because it relaxes the anal muscles (more about this later). In general, breath helps the whole body to relax, while focusing on conscious breathing takes you out of your mind. This allows you to let go of anxiety-laden messages that may exacerbate the rapidity of your ejaculation, such as, "She's going to be pissed if I come quickly" or "I'm going to screw it up again."

These messages put your body into a high level of stress and tension, your breathing becomes shallower and your muscles automatically tense. All of these thoughts distance you from your body, taking you out of connection with your own sensation. Orgasming and ejaculating in this state can feel unsatisfying and emotionally, or even physically, painful. Breath helps you relax into the experience, it helps you slow down and feel and enjoy the pleasure throughout the experience.

Relax Your Ass

The term "tight-ass" is not a metaphor. When your body is anxious, stressed, angry or in a hurry, you literally clench the muscles in your ass. What you might not realize is that ejaculation creates an involuntary clenching of the anal muscles. If, when you go into a sexual experience, your anal muscles are already clenched, you are heading toward an ejaculation before you even begin. This is why it is essential to get in touch with the muscles in your ass and learn to relax them. Some positions, such as the missionary position, make it much more likely that your anal muscles tighten with each thrust. These positions require much more conscious awareness of what your anal muscles are doing.

The most relaxing position for the anal muscles is probably woman-on-top. However, if she is controlling the thrusting motion, this can make it more difficult for you to have control over the timing and amount of stimulation. Other positions to try are spooning or doggie-style where you can move in and out of her with less anal muscle tightening. Throughout any sexual experience be consciously aware of breathing. Relax the tension in your asshole. If you are not sure whether your muscles are clenched, you can feel them with your fingers.

Learn Your Arousal Curve

Next, it is important that you are in touch with your arousal curve. To get in touch with your own arousal curve, picture your arousal existing on a scale from one to ten, where zero is not aroused at all, one is very slightly aroused and ten is the point of no return. Many men who desire better control say that shortly after they enter their partner's vagina, their arousal suddenly spikes and they orgasm and ejaculate. This is doubly unfortunate because they feel as though they are disappointing their partner by not lasting long enough and also do not last long enough to build their own level of pleasure.

Many men who complain about early ejaculation either have difficulty identifying where they are on their arousal curve or they know where they are but jump immediately from three to nine without ever visiting the intermediate levels. Suddenly, they are coming and they have no idea how they got there so quickly. The idea here is for you to get in touch with each step of your arousal curve so you know where you are at any point in your sexual experience.

Men who are early ejaculators often experience a sudden rush to orgasm without much consciousness of the sensations leading up to it. As you get in touch with your arousal curve, you can take a slower path to high arousal. By breathing, going slowly and enjoying foreplay, you can spend more time in lower arousal states, consciously acknowledging the sensations and feelings before proceeding into a higher arousal. Then you can "float" in the comfortable but high arousal state for at least a few minutes before ejaculating. This practice can lead to the ideal, in which a high arousal state can be reached and then maintained almost indefinitely, or until you decide you are ready to orgasm.

Find the Sweet Spot

The "sweet spot" is between an arousal level of six and eight. The great thing about the sweet spot is that you experience a lot of pleasure and sensation so hanging out there can be really sexually satisfying, allows you to build sexual energy in your body, and keeps you erect throughout the experience. Once you get to the sweet spot, it is also possible to engage even more deeply in the connection with your partner. Eventually, you can learn to surf the sweet spot for as long as you like before coming.

Expand Your Masturbation Practice

One of the most effective ways to move towards true mastery of your sexual function and experience the heights of what is sexually possible for you is to expand your masturbation practice.

By the time boys first discover masturbation, they have likely gotten the message that sex was something they were supposed to hide, or, at the very least, to do privately. Because these experiences were supposed to be hidden, boys often rushed to the conclusion instead of taking time to enjoy the building and spreading of pleasure in their body. Since masturbation is the earliest and most directly relevant training your body gets about how it will be sexually later on in your life, rushed early masturbation experiences are generally the beginning of a long-term pattern of hurried ejaculation.

Expanded masturbation is one practice that can bring you closer to the experience of a full-body orgasm as well as non-ejaculatory orgasms. The fact is, in both men and women, orgasm and ejaculation are two different bodily functions. You can learn to separate them if you are interested in taking the time and energy to do so. The payoff for taking the time is that non-ejaculatory orgasms allow you to be multi-orgasmic because the hormones that cause you to lose your erection are not released until you ejaculate.

Six great ways to expand your masturbation practice are:

1. Deep breathing.
2. Touching all of your body in different ways.
3. Moving your body or changing positions.
4. Making sound.
5. Watching yourself in the mirror (especially during orgasm).
6. Trying different kinds of lubrication during masturbation.

Empower Your Erection

There are many physiological reasons why you might have difficulty getting an erection. Many health conditions and medications can affect your ability, including diabetes and hypertension medication. If you are having trouble getting and maintaining erections in all situations including masturbation and partner sex, it is always a good idea to get a medical check up since research has recently shown that the inability to get an erection can be an early sign of heart disease.

On the other hand, many men are able to have a normal erection when they masturbate and then cannot get hard in a sexual situation with a partner. In this case, erectile difficulties are usually more psychological. Also, as men get into their thirties and forties, or at the beginning of a sexual relationship with a new woman, it is normal for their erections to go up and down. As men age, the overall hardness of erections can also lessen. Usually, with erection difficulties you start to get erect and then, if it goes down slightly, you go into performance anxiety and negative self-talk that exacerbates the problem. As your confidence drops and your anxiety level goes up you go into a mild to medium fight/flight response and the blood moves from your genitals to your chest and stomach, depleting your erection.

In order to get the most out of your erection follow these steps:

- **Take the pressure off your cock.** Cocks get so much pressure in our society to get hard immediately or stay hard all the time. This pressure is exacerbated by porn, which shows unrealistic portrayals of drug-enhanced erections and cuts in the film any time an erection is lost.
- **Use the Let Go of Performance exercises.** Because so many erectile difficulties are caused and made worse by performance anxiety, getting more connected with your body in the ways we

suggest around performance anxiety are the best place to start with erectile difficulties. Focusing on your breath to reconnect with your body and erotic energy as well as focusing on sensations – the subtleties of touching and being touched as well as the smells, sounds and tastes of the experience – will help you most with your erection.

♦ **Replace negative thoughts.** If, during sex, you find yourself saying inside your head "I'm never going to get erect" or "Don't lose your erection," try replacing them with thoughts like, "Sometimes my erection comes and goes," or "It's ok to relax and enjoy myself, whatever happens we can both have tons of pleasure."

♦ **Explore the underlying emotional causes.** How are you feeling in your sexual relationship? How is your attraction to your partner? How is your sexual communication? Is the sex you are having the kind of sex you most enjoy?

♦ **Consider trying a performance-enhancing drug.** If you are feeling very anxious and nothing else is working, try Cialis or Viagra. If you do choose to take these pills, try them for a while to gain confidence back while at the same time continuing to work on deepening your embodiment so you won't have to rely on them forever.

Remember, erections often come and go and erections

that go down can come back up, but, more than anything, women want to feel something during sex. Women can be very forgiving and patient around erections as long as you are bringing them desire, sensuality, intensity and passion (more on this in the second section of the book).

The confidence of connecting with other men, feeling yourself as an equal without comparing, being in touch with your body and mastering your sexual function are all tremendous steps towards *Cockfidence*. While confidence sounds a lot like *Cockfidence*, it is just one of the nine qualities of *Cockfidence* – it is also an important quality to have so that you can develop the other eight.

EXERCISE
Embodied Confidence Reprogramming

You can do this exercise literally by taking part in an activity that you are very adept at or going to a place where you feel your deepest sense of confidence. You can also use your imagination and remember an experience you had in which you felt like you were at the very top of your game. Maybe you were playing basketball or piano, or teaching a skill like snowboarding to someone who had never done it before.

Perhaps you remember a time or place where you realized that you could do something extremely well, so well that you or others were in awe of this ability. It may even be a time or place where you felt extremely physically strong or competent. Either literally visit that place again or go there in your mind. If you choose to delve into this memory, it is not helpful if you just use your conscious mind. To really feel the feeling in your body again, you must do it in a mindful way.

Use the following steps:

◆ Find a comfortable place where your body is supported and begin with Sexual Embodiment Breath, breathing at least twenty deep breaths in and out through your mouth.

◆ Breathe all the way down to your pelvic floor and allow your mind to become gentle, relaxed and empty.

◆ If random thoughts come through, notice them and allow them to float away.

◆ Gently let your mind travel back to a place where you felt yourself most confident, competent or powerful. Choose one specific memory or moment, not a set or series of memories.

◆ Once you have landed on a particular memory, begin to paint every detail of the memory.

  - Notice where you are and who is there with you.

  - Notice the time, the location, the weather.

  - Notice sounds, sights, smells.

  - Notice what you and others are wearing.

◆ Let yourself flow through the entire experience with your eyes closed and your body relaxed.

◆ Allow the sensations of confidence to fill your body.

Once you have moved through the whole memory, take note of how you feel in your body and ask yourself the following questions:

- Is your breath deep and open?
- Can you feel your arms and legs?
- What is your posture like in the memory?
- How do you sit, stand or walk?
- When you look around, how do you feel about your surroundings?
- How do you imagine others are feeling about you?

When you find the place of relaxed arousal and comfort in your body, you have found embodied confidence. It is not something that you can fake by standing up straight or memorizing a bunch of witty pick-up lines. It happens only when you really feel it in your body.

Generosity

enerosity is the act of giving wholeheartedly of yourself - and your resources - for the joy of giving and *without expecting reciprocation*. It is the sentence, "I am offering you this not because I feel obligated or want you to feel obligated, but because it feels good inside me to give it."

Give What You Enjoy Giving

Let's take two looks at a potentially generous offering, the backrub. The first approach is to offer a backrub as a way to get to sex. You half-heartedly knead and rub her shoulders trying to figure out how quickly you can begin touching her butt, kissing her neck and getting between her legs.

The second approach is to give a woman a backrub because you feel generous and enjoy seeing her feel relaxed.

You take your time, noticing what parts of her body respond and relax under your touch. You enjoy each stroke that you are offering. If it leads to sex, great, if not, great! If it is a truly generous backrub, you will feel her pleasure in your own body. Both the giver and receiver can feel the same physical pleasure from the same backrub - we talk more about this when we talk about empathy.

Anyone can feel the difference between these two kinds of giving and only one of these approaches is generous. Women, and people in general, know whether you are giving in order to get something or giving for the joy of giving – and they respond in kind. In the long-term, giving in order to get spells the death of passion and kills the flow of genuine, internally-motivated offerings. When you are generous because you want to be, you increase your own sense of freedom and power, you become *Cockfident*. You are giving because it feels good to give. By doing this, you encourage the flow of desire, connection, affection, intimacy and passion between you and a partner.

Growing up, many boys saw their parents and other close adults, filled with pressure and an expectation to provide, give to their families out of obligation. Fathers stayed in tedious jobs they hated and dealt with their partner's and children's needs because that was what they were "supposed" to do. Mothers gave up their dreams and desires and did everything for the sake of their children. These role models generally ranged from resigned to resentful and angry. They were certainly neither free nor powerful.

Boys who grew up with the message that they were supposed to put their own needs, feelings, goals and desires aside in the name of obligation often turn into men who give from a place of obligation. They slowly, and often unconsciously, build resentment and frustration along the way. As they continue along the path of obligation, these men begin to feel deprived and unfulfilled.

At the same time, many men experience a feeling of scarcity around women; they are afraid that women only want them for what they can give or they fear they will never find another woman if they lose the one they have. In the face of this perceived scarcity, they attempt to maintain the relationship by giving or doing things that they don't want to do. When you are giving out of scarcity and obligation you lose true generosity. Worse, this kind of giving often leads to resentment.

When you stay true to your own goals and desires and give from love instead of obligation, you are free, powerful and emotionally available to your partner because you are being who you really are. This is why it is essential to learn how to give out of generosity.

There is an easy way to tell that you are giving from a place of generosity as opposed to obligation. When you are in the act of giving, breathe deeply and tune in to what it feels like in your body in the moment. *If you are feeling light and excited during the experience, then you know you are giving from generosity;* if you feel a sense of heaviness, exhaustion or frustration, you are giving out of obligation.

The tricky part about giving out of obligation is that it can seem like it feels good because you can get a lot of positive reinforcement. For example, working at a job you hate day in and day out may get you consistent appreciation from your partner, but the actual sensations that you have during the hours and hours you spend at work are oppressive and painful. Over time, your life gets more and more unbearable as you feel less and less freedom to live your life the way that you want to. The same can happen in your sex life. Being an Extraodinary Lover and a *Cockfident* man means listening to your body as you give.

This is why it is essential to pay attention to how it feels in your body to give *in the moment* and not evaluate your generosity based on other's gratitude or outside positive reinforcement. Only you can know whether it feels good based on your own physiological experience of giving. So be aware, when you feel that genuine, generous feeling welling up, use it. Offer your partner a flower, grab her and kiss her or say, "I'm so crazy about you."

Know Your Boundaries

Having boundaries means having an ongoing right to choose what you want and don't want at any moment. An essential part of generosity is knowing, communicating and sticking by your boundaries. When you stick by your own boundaries, you can give generously without building resentment. Imagine that you are doing something for someone you care about and, at the end of doing it, you feel like saying, "I'm so hurt and angry, I did so much for you and you have done nothing for me." If you have gotten to this point, *you have crossed your own boundaries* by giving beyond your own level of comfort.

Resentment comes when you give (or compromise) beyond your comfort zone and resentment is the #1 killer of long-term relationships. The more you build resentment and blame your partner for "making" you do things you don't want to do or give up things you truly want, the more you distance from her. Unless she is holding a gun to your head, she is not "making" you do anything - you are doing it of your own choice and volition.

Boundaries are the basis of generosity. They require that you give only as much as you want to give and only accept behaviors from your partner that feel comfortable for you. In this way, they lead to a deep sense of personal power.

Boundaries are also the foundation of your partner's trust for you. If your partner knows that you will not compromise yourself or your own needs in order to fulfill hers, she can feel safe in knowing you aren't sitting across from her stewing in resentment, getting depressed or getting ready to explode or leave. She can trust that you take care of yourself and communicate your own needs and limits. It is actually a generous act to maintain your own boundaries and respecting her boundaries is profoundly generous as well.

Often, people confuse boundaries with barriers. Barriers keep people out based on a fear that to let someone in means losing yourself; boundaries are an assertion of self that says, "This is what I am comfortable with right now." If you are true to your boundaries, you develop a trust for yourself because you know that you can let another person be close to you without losing your freedom. Boundaries allow other people to trust you because, by keeping your boundaries, you are essentially telling your partner, "I am responsible for taking care of myself throughout this process."

Face Conflict

Growing up, most of us learned that conflict was something to avoid. We rarely saw people in positive conversations about difficult topics, and culturally, we do not air our "dirty laundry." Parents usually keep their difficult conversations hidden from their children, or yell and scream and act out in front of them, but rarely do they allow their children to be privy to healthy conflict. Men also feel a strong obligation to make their partners happy so they avoid anything that upsets their partner.

Both men and women refrain from communicating their needs and boundaries in relationships because they fear the momentary distance or hurt that asking for something or saying "no" might trigger in their partner. Seeing your partner hurt or distant from you can be very uncomfortable, especially if you are not confident in the strength of your connection.

However, tolerance for this temporary distance increases the likelihood that you can stay close with your partner. When you face conflict head on by asserting your boundaries, you can get closer to the people you care about because getting close does not mean that you have to lose yourself.

When you say something like, "Yes, I really like you and want to continue seeing you but I am not ready to be in a committed relationship right now" or "I know you are really upset, but I need to take a break from talking about it and come back to it later," then you are taking care of yourself and asking for what you need in order to keep the connection intact. You are generously giving both parties in the relationship – you and her – the gift of honesty and respect.

Learn to Say and Hear "No"

One of the most difficult and essential steps that people who care about each other can take is learning how to say "no" without feeling mean and to hear "no" without feeling rejected. Everyone has boundaries; if you think you don't you are lying to yourself. At the most extreme, for example, it would not be okay with you if your partner wanted to chop off your hand. Now that we have your first boundary established, it is time to go further. If you've never said to friends, parents or women you've been with "You can't treat me like that," "That is not fair" or "I don't want to do that, I'd rather _____" then it is time to start. If you don't communicate your "no" then there is some part of yourself that you are hiding away and keeping from your relationship. In very important ways, you are not really in the relationship at all.

Sometimes men don't say "no" because they fear hearing "no." They fear that if they are really true to what they want and don't want, their partner might act in kind and begin to advocate for what she really wants as well. This is a valid and exciting fear to face; it might be that part of your dating or relationship agreement is that each of you endures all sorts of things you don't want in order to maintain the relationship. Encouraging your partner to find her boundaries helps her more fully engage in all of her experiences with you. When each person lives according to his or her desires and boundaries the relationship stays exciting and connected because you continue to grow, change, and be generous with one another.

Pass Women's Tests

People test each other all the time in relationship trying to get as much as possible and to find out what their partners are made of. Any woman that you are with will consciously or unconsciously test your boundaries and your self-respect. When she feels your boundaries, she will allow herself to open up, knowing that you are able to take care of yourself and be a powerful container for her emotional journey. If you always go along with what she wants she might seem content with your ac-quiescence and with you taking everything she dishes out but *she will not respect you or maintain her attrac-tion to you if she doesn't feel the power of your boundaries.* A *Cockfident* man offers his boundaries as a part of his generosity – though it may seem counterintuitive, being true to yourself and maintaining boundaries is perhaps the most generous act you can make because boundaries create safety. Having boundaries means that you don't just go along with everything while slowly getting less and less happy inside.

When you communicate your boundaries and keep them in response to a woman's testing, it creates trust in the relationship. If she knows that you maintain your boundaries, she can relax, knowing that you are responsible for your needs. Many men (and women) do not communicate their needs and boundaries, waiting for a partner who will intuit their needs instead of asserting themselves.

If you assert your boundaries and allow that there may be some distance in that moment, when you come back together, you will have learned more about each other and deepened intimacy and connection in the relationship. If you ignore your boundaries, you take a step away from the relationship. Eventually, to be yourself again, you will either need to leave, to stay and lie, or to stay and shut down. Many women have gone through this before. Whether they are conscious of it or not, they know the warning signs well, which is why they test your boundaries.

One common consequence of men not asking for what they want is an affair. Men often go to affairs to regain a sense of freedom and fulfillment. In the affair men get the feeling "She lets me be everything that I want to be" instead of claiming their freedom in their own relationship. If you go to an affair, this freedom is generally temporary because the underlying behavior – not keeping your boundaries – has not changed. If you are willing to be strong and communicate what you want and need, you can create a relationship that works for you and desire, generosity, and passion can flourish.

Practice Complete Honesty to Build Trust

When you communicate your boundaries, you build trust and this trust creates the opportunity for longevity in relationship. The best sex and relationships happen when people feel most free and honestly generous. Often in relationships, men don't feel free to share all of who they are with their partners. Relationships often begin as giant marketing campaigns. You try to put your best foot forward and hope that the person you are dating or falling in love with is everything you want them to be and that you can be everything for them. In the long term, this marketing campaign can result in never fully revealing all of who you are and what you want for fear that you might feel disappointed, that you might disappoint your partner or that no one can really love you if they know everything.

We invite you to imagine what it would be like to have a truly honest relationship with a lover. Instead of hiding what you want or pretending everything is okay, you ask for it with the clear knowledge that you won't always get it. You talk about who you are while knowing that your partner won't always like it and encourage your partner to do the same. It turns out that the strongest relationships are those where each person is allowed to experience the inevitable disappointment that their partner is not going to be everything they want them to be and have it acknowledged. These strong relationships also make room for each person in the partnership to ask for what they want and to say and hear either "yes" or "no."

Men (and women) often justify lying by pointing out the things in the relationship they are resentful of. "She never wants to do anything exciting sexually, so occasionally I pick up someone and have hot sex with them. Don't get me wrong, I don't want to leave my wife, I just want the sex to be hot and fun." Rarely, in this situation, has the man said to his wife, "Look, there are deeply important parts of me that I am unable to share with you in this relationship because I think that you do not want to do anything wild with me sexually. These are parts of myself that are essential and that I do not want to lose. I want to share them with you." Again, she may not be able to do it, but at least this way she has an opportunity to see how essential it is to you and how unhappy it makes you. It opens the possibility for communication and negotiation. When you do not communicate your deepest needs with your partner, you have taken away her choice and, if you are lying and cheating and it is found out, you have undermined the potential for trust to ever fully return to the relationship. Being honest is being generous with your feelings and desire, which is a service to your partner, but even more importantly, it honors who you are and what you want.

EXERCISES
Start with Low-Stakes Boundaries

If you haven't had a lot of practice with boundaries, the thought of setting tough boundaries or being open about your deepest needs with a lover may feel like a huge leap. If this is the case, we invite you to practice in a low stakes way. In most of our day-to-day interactions with everyone from family members to store clerks, we have many opportunities to say what we need or to turn down things we don't want. Instead of being polite and saying yes to offerings that you are not interested in, try practicing being clear while still being kind.

Here are a few not-too-serious examples that we'd like you to take seriously:

- Every time you go to visit your mom, she puts twice as much food on your plate than you'd like and then is upset when you don't eat it all. So, you buckle down and stuff it in. Instead of suffering from your mom's overfeeding, next time before dinner, tell her that you'd like half as much, that you'd prefer to serve yourself or that you are only going to eat until you are full.

- Every week your sweetheart wants you to sit with her and watch a line-up of her favorite situation comedies. You can make it through Modern Family, but Cougar Town nearly kills you. Tell her you'd be happy to watch Modern Family, but you are going to sit out Cougar Town. It's also a great practice to say these things sweetly; you'll find you can be much nicer when you aren't doing a bunch of things you don't want to do. Try saying something like, "I'd love to watch Modern Family with you tonight, and I love hearing you laugh at Cougar Town, but I'm going to take the time to do some reading while you watch it."

- You have this one friend who calls you every week and tells you about all the women he's supposedly slept with and you are sick of it. Tell him that you are really happy for all of his ongoing conquests, but that you'd rather talk about something else and give him some options for topics that would be of more interest to you.

As you are setting boundaries with those you are close to, bring awareness to how it feels to set them. Notice how it feels in your body to say no or to ask for what you'd actually like to do and answer the following questions:

- What parts of it feel uncomfortable or unfamiliar?
- Can you stay close and connected with people as you ask for what you need or do you feel like you have to shut them out emotionally in order to set boundaries?
- What parts of setting boundaries make you feel more free and powerful?

Giving a Generous Backrub

Since we began with the example of a backrub, we figured it would be a great place to help you practice giving for your own pleasure. The tools you use to give a generous backrub can be used to offer anything generously. Hopefully, since you have just read the section on boundaries, saying this is redundant, but we'll say it anyway – if you can't find anything you like about giving a backrub, *don't give one.* If, after reading these suggestions, backrubs still hold no interest for you, take a moment and imagine something fun that you'd like to give that you think your partner would like to receive from you; use this backrub example as a basic guideline.

◆ **Make an open offer** – Offer the backrub without any need for your partner to want what you are giving. If she wants it great; if not, great! If the refusal of a backrub seems to be coming from built up resentment, it would be best for you to elicit and hear your partner's emotions (Quality 6: Empathy). If she accepts your generous offer, take charge.

◆ **Take charge** – Decide if you will be guiding the process or if you'd rather invite her to do it. If either sounds great to you, ask her whether she'd like to give suggestions or just lie back and enjoy. Regardless, do it the way you want to do it.

◆ **Tune into your body** – Whether she is asking for what she wants or you are offering your spontaneous gifts, pay attention to what the sensation of giving feels like in your body. Notice your hands and fingertips as you rub, notice how her body's responses resonate in your own body. Notice what kinds of touch feel good to give.

◆ **Take care of yourself** – Only give to the point that you feel comfortable giving. If you are in the mood for a fifteen-minute backrub, stop after fifteen minutes. If you could do it all night long, let her tell you when she's had enough. If she wants deeper pressure and your wrists are killing you, give her as much pressure as you can while still staying comfortable in your own body.

◆ **Have fun** – Let your creativity flow. When you are in the moment of generosity, wonderful, passionate, playful exchanges of energy are possible. Give yourself room to let the full force of your personality out in the giving and feel the freedom and power of this truly generous gift.

Passion

Passion is the deeply sensed and embodied feeling that you are truly inspired by a person, activity, goal or desire. In sexual situations, women want to feel the force of your desire for them and the intensity of sensation that desire creates in your body. It is the sentence, "I want you so badly right now, I would do anything to have you." This is different than saying, "I would do anything for you." It is not sexy to enslave yourself to women or put them on a pedestal. The sentiment of passion is one of raw, animalistic desire, as in, "My passion is so strong right now, I can barely contain myself."

To really excite and intrigue any woman, you need to be passionate about more than just her; you need to begin to look at your whole life through passionate eyes. If you are currently living your life based on what you should do instead of what interests or intrigues you, it is time to find your own path that excites and inspires you, and to support the women in your life in finding their passion too. It is possible to bring passion into every part of your life, and a *Cockfident* man feels passion for his work flowing into passion for his hobbies, flowing into passion for his partner.

Live a Life of Passion

Do you remember what you wanted to be when you grew up? As a boy, there were probably many activities and topics you were passionate about and we hope there still are. If, in the time it took to read this last paragraph about passion, you haven't already identified three things you are passionate about (not including your partner if you have one), then it is time for you to reacquaint yourself with your passionate side. Your sense of freedom and power rests on your ability to enjoy your own life and give your gift to the world. There is nothing more attractive than someone who is willing to follow through with what they truly believe. Notice if you are judging any of your passions as trivial or discounting them. Notice whose voices are in your head naysaying or criticizing.

Just for a moment, see if you can suspend the judgmental voice and remember what you are passionate about. You might also think about how your family of origin responded to ideas or desires that inspired you and how they communicated their expectations.

Take some time to ponder or write on the following questions:

- What is a topic that you could talk about for hours without tiring?
- What activities do you do that make you feel more like yourself?
- What are things that you do for your friends or family that make you feel most proud and content?
- What ideas and experiences grab your interest and make your heart beat faster?

Now check what percentage of your life is spent in the pursuit of these activities, ideas and experiences. Is it enough? Only you know the answer to this question, only you can decide what you want your life to look like, and only you can know the right way to live your life.

Revel in the Enjoyment of Your Desire

Men rarely have a chance to develop a true enjoyment of their own desire as an essential part of their masculinity. Early on, you were given messages from parents, friends, television, religious institutions and schools about both men's and women's sexuality. As boys, you probably got the message, at least covertly, that men are sexual and that this sexuality is a natural, animalistic drive. At the same time, you may have gotten the message that this drive is overpowering, wrong, and dangerous and that you have to learn how to temper and control it. In other situations, you may have been given the message you should go out and exercise this drive as much as you want to. You should "sow your wild oats" and "play the field."

At the same time, both you and the girls around you were told that girls are not really sexual people. We cover how this affects women's sexuality later, but the most important element of this when it comes to passion is that men are often told that their sexual drive will not be received or reciprocated by women. In your own life, the combination of these two messages – that boys have an overpowering, animalistic sexuality and that girls are basically without a sexual drive – most likely led you to feel at least some level of discomfort with your sexuality. At worst, it caused you to lose touch with your own sexual power and confidence in your desires.

Your desires for women, sex, and pleasure are the most natural desires you have – they are built into your body in order for the species to survive and they are foundational to passion. However, often when men feel desire and they have been told that it is wrong, the desire makes them anxious. As soon as desire arises, they feel like they have to *do* something about it.

The next time you see a gorgeous woman that turns you on, try standing up straight, taking a deep breath, and feeling your desire flow through your body. Feel how good it feels that you still have this desire in your body; it means that you are alive and inspired. It is really not about her and there is nothing to *do* about it. Feeling your desire and allowing it actually creates a magnetism that invites women into the field of your passion. If you aren't afraid of your desire, women won't be afraid of it either.

Take Women Off the Pedestal

Putting a woman on a pedestal means thinking of her as out-of-reach or unattainable. The pedestal comes from the terrible set-up we have in our culture in which women are supposed to be pure and non-sexual and are given the responsibility of gatekeeping sexuality. This is a negative set up for both men and women. Women distance themselves from their own sexual desires, and men feel a sense of frustration and scarcity when they believe that women don't want sex. Women do not choose to be the sexual gatekeepers, but end up dealing with all of the negative consequences of this role, including not being able to really connect with and enjoy their own sexuality or think about and ask for what they want. One very negative consequence for women is that they are placed on a pedestal. *Despite what you might be told, this is a bad thing* – for them and you.

Putting women on a pedestal takes away men's opportunity to have true intimacy and passion with them.

Men feel powerless in the situation, believing that women are not within reach. This becomes a self-fulfilling prophecy because women are turned off by your powerlessness. When you realize that women are sexual creatures, that they are accessible, and they want what you have to offer, you can take them off the pedestal and meet them as an equal partner.

Explore Your Dominant Side

Many men feel deeply ambivalent about the idea of dominance. Dominance is feeling comfortable asserting your desires clearly and straightforwardly with an expectation of being received. It is also a willingness to take the lead and be directive in social and sexual situations. When you are assertive and directive about your desire, you may or may not be received, but expecting that you won't be is the surest way to rejection. Embracing the dominant part of yourself allows you to feel more yourself and more connected with your drive and your passion. Your dominant side has nothing to do with other people's responses. It is about truly getting to know, accept and express yourself and your desires.

There are at least three unhelpful ways that men relate to their dominant side:

1. **Avoid Dominance** – You may avoid your dominant side completely, especially if you have experienced abusive men in your life. You may totally

divorce yourself from this part by feeling or saying, "I'm just not that kind of guy." We have heard so many men like this complain, "I don't get it, why do women always pick the jerks? What do I have to do, stop calling women back or put them down or what?" Again, a woman does not ultimately want to date someone who treats her badly but she will sometimes chose to because of the confidence he projects. Women look for very different things in male friends and male lovers. Appearing safe, friendly, and sweet can allow you to ingratiate yourself as a friend, but it is unlikely to get you many hot, excited lovers. Practicing dominance can help you show your desire from the very beginning and keep yourself out of the friend category.

2. **Dwell on Dominance** – Another relationship you may have with your dominant side is to dwell on it. You may fantasize or watch porn with these themes in it and you might think, "Yeah, these kinds of fantasies are always in the back of my mind, but no woman would ever accept that part of me. And, if she does, there is something wrong with her."

3. **Become Abusive** – Some men who feel powerless in their own lives or are very fearful may take a third path – becoming abusive, either physically or emotionally. The experience is, "I don't know

what to do with these feelings of powerlessness, so I get angry and hurt others or put others down." Exploring your dominant side is never about abusing or doing anything that is non-consensual. Abuse is an out of control urge for dominance that comes from prior abuse, suppression and fear.

Integrating your dominant side is an important step on the path to power, fearlessness and a satisfying sex life. It allows you to truly share your sexuality with a partner who can fully receive it and allows you to experience the full depth of satisfaction available to you, without guilt or shame.

If you have never explored your dominant side, it can be difficult to access this part of yourself. While dominance is not abusive, the pure energy of anger can help you connect with your dominance. Often, with men who have never explored their dominant side, we invite them to just connect with a little bit of anger in their body and bring it into the mix, perhaps ten to twenty percent. Anger in the sexual arena acts as an energetic motivator and counters some of your tendencies to try to make women like you or to come across as a "good guy."

Until you have actually gone into the bodily experience of dominance, you can have no idea what it holds for you. When you first play in this arena, you may feel adrenaline rush through your body. It may make your body shake and you may want to pull away from it. You might have feelings of fear or deep emotions may arise. At the same time, if you have spent hours and hours dwelling on it and feeling guilty and shameful, you may find that it is not as big of a deal as you thought it was. By integrating your dominant side, you may feel a level of security with yourself that you never knew you had available to you. This sense of confidence enhances your personal power in every area of your life, including your business relationships.

Most importantly, you may also find that it can be very hot for both you and your partner and it can open up a whole other arena in which to play. We explore more ways to play with dominance when we discuss the Dominant Seduction Movie in the second section.

Clarify Your Relationship to Porn

As a result of the Internet, pornographic movies are more prevalent than they have been at any other time in history. There are many plusses and minuses to porn, so, in the interest of time, we want to start out by saying that porn can be a wonderful addition to a single person's or a couple's sexual life. However, the excessive use of porn can get in the way of passionate connections with real-life sexual partners.

It is important to consciously understand and clarify your relationship to pornography in order to avoid some of its downsides. Many folks have talked and written about the problems of porn, but these discussions are mostly in terms of its social implications (i.e., questioning whether or not it is harmful to women, etc.) Here, we want to talk about some of the challenges of porn in terms of how it affects your relationship with women, your fantasy life, and your sexual function.

Take some time to think about how you approach the question of porn in your relationships with women. Is it something that you want to do privately, just for you? Is it something that you want to talk with your partner about, but not share? Is it something that you want to share with your partner by watching it together and watch it privately as well? Do you want to only share it with your partner once you enter into a relationship and stop watching it privately?

Each of these choices is valid and each has different implications and potential outcomes for your relationship. For example, most women know that men watch porn, so, if you choose not to talk about your porn watching, it could feel secretive and uncomfortable. On the other hand, some women are very uncomfortable with the idea that their partners watch porn and a certain amount of privacy can be very healthy in relationships.

Even if a woman you are seeing says her discomfort is for political reasons, she probably has her own personal feelings around porn. The main political reasons women don't like porn is because they feel it is degrading to women. The main personal reason women don't like porn is because they feel it is just one more way that they are being compared to women who may seem more desirable than they feel they are.

Your partner's response to you watching porn may make you feel judged so it is important to deal with any of your own personal feelings of guilt or shame around watching porn. No matter how you choose to proceed in terms of communication, there are a few suggestions that we want to make around porn that can enhance your ability to have passionate sexual connections with women.

Reclaim Your Fantasy Life

One of the biggest challenges that come from the proliferation of porn has to do with men losing the creativity that comes from exploring their own fantasy images. Many men watch porn every time they masturbate and are unable to get excited enough by their own personal fantasies to masturbate without porn. This affects both their sexual creativity and their flexibility in terms of what kinds of experiences are going to turn them on in their real-life sexual encounters.

If you watch porn all the time, and, especially if you focus on one particular type of porn, you begin to limit the types of thoughts, experiences and images that excite you, narrowing your sexual spectrum. You also lose touch with the power of your own sexual imagination. We strongly suggest at the very least that you diversify the types of porn that you watch.

To reclaim your fantasies, we suggest you spend at least some of your masturbation time porn-free so that you can rediscover and explore your own imagination. You may need to be patient with this as it may take some time to retrain your body to respond to these internal images. Once you do, however, this imagination can be a very powerful tool towards discovering who you are and what you want as a sexual person.

Make Your Own "Sensational" Porn

Another potentially negative ramification of porn that you may want to consider is a long-term reduction in sensation. The reason porn reduces sensation in the body is because it basically bypasses the body's natural biological arousal process, often putting you immediately to the brink of orgasm with very little bodily stimulation. It also focuses almost entirely on visual stimulation, leaving the other senses behind. We see many men coming into our practice after years of porn-inspired masturbation who have difficulties being sexual with their own partners; either they are unable to get an erection, they ejaculate very quickly or they are unable to get to climax without porn.

We have a fun, playful solution that you might try with

your sweetheart or with yourself. We call it "Sensational Porn." It's time for you to be director, screenwriter and actor, so engage your imagination and create a sexy, sensational, and passionate experience. Porn's intensity is often mistaken for passion, but it is generally void of real feelings. Now is your chance to add passion to porn! If you are feeling really adventurous, you might even want to make a video. Some women may feel wary about making a sexy movie with you. If your partner is worried, one thing you can do is give her all the "rights" to the movie. In other words, you can let her keep the tape or the file. As for the rest, the plot, the action, and the dialogue can be all yours or it can be co-created.

To make your sexual experiences truly sensational, the only thing we suggest is that, somewhere in the experience, every part of your body (or bodies) is touched, kissed, scratched, stroked, tickled, bitten, spanked or teased. If you're masturbating, you can touch and tease yourself all over using different kinds of stimulators – including massagers, back scratchers, soft materials and more. Make sure you engage all of your senses. Bring something scented like a candle, something that tastes good, and good music (or you and your partner can make your own sexy sounds). Put a blindfold on and just feel, smell, taste, hear and touch. Take time to feel your entire body, touch your partner's entire body and let her touch yours. Don't chase the orgasm, let the orgasm come to you.

Sensational sex enhances the long-term health of your arousal and sexual response. We certainly aren't suggesting that people need to quit watching porn, though it might be a good idea to give yourself a little all-over body foreplay before you turn on your favorite movie. And again, we suggest you watch a wide variety of porn to keep your brain open to multiple turn-ons. You might be surprised at what new imagery turns you on!

If you do decide to make an actual movie with your own sexual partners, there is another fantastic benefit. It keeps your sexual partner as one of the centers of your sexual fantasies and may help her feel less jealous or insecure about you watching other types of porn.

Break the Habit

At its most destructive, porn can become a habitual behavior, can be used to avoid painful emotions and can shut men out from experiencing passion, true intimacy or erotic energy exchange with their partners. You know you are addicted to porn if the amount of pornography or the type of pornography you watch has negative ramifications in your life, based on *your* definition. In other words, if you watch a few hours a day of porn but are perfectly happy with your life, still go to and enjoy your work, still maintain close relationships with women, family and friends, then you might not define this amount of porn watching as a problem.

If, on the other hand, your watching of porn all night means you rarely make it to work on time, often have low energy or call in sick, cannot have sexual pleasure with a partner unless porn is involved or no longer get turned on by your real life partner(s), then you might become unhappy with this habit and want to make some kind of change in your life around it. Like any other emotion-avoiding habit, a habitual relationship to porn can be difficult to quit and you may require the help of a professional. We have worked with many men to help them change habitual porn-watching. There are five easy places to start:

1. **Stop beating yourself up.** Most habits are tied up in a shame/guilt cycle, but nothing good ever comes from beating yourself up.

2. **Re-read Listening to Your Emotions and do the exercise Tracking Your Emotions in Quality 2.** Feel your feelings, acknowledge them and let them release instead of avoiding them with porn.

3. **Take all of the pornography out of your house.** For a while, you may even need to forgo having a home internet connection in order to quit the habit.

4. **Practice sensation-based and fantasy-based masturbation.**

5. **Get out of the house.** Spend as much time as possible doing activities you like or being with people you enjoy being around.

Passion Needs Distance and Change

A final note on passion for those of you in long-term relationships: passion needs distance across which to travel. The fires of passion are stoked by uncertainty and are hottest when questions like "Does he/she want me?" and "Are we going to be together?" are still part of the equation. This is why passion is usually highest at the beginning of a relationship and why it wanes over time. If you have spent a long time with someone in a committed relationship and life feels settled, you are quite likely to lose the level of passion you once felt for a person. Spontaneous desire for sex can drop and people long for it but don't know how to re-ignite it.

One way to keep passion high in the relationship is to continue to pursue other passions in your life having to do with work and with personal growth. If your partner knows everything about you and you spend all of your time together, there is no distance. However, if you are growing, changing and following your passions, and sharing these changes with your partner, your relationship can continue to be new and fresh. In addition, to keep passion alive, you need to take a different approach to sex than hoping that it will just happen spontaneously all the time. You need to be creative and play with distance by exploring new sexual experiences, new fantasies and new desires with your partner. We give you in-depth ideas for exploration in the second part of this book!

EXERCISE
Throw Her Against the Wall

One of the most fun and enlightening experiences we have in our coaching with men is when we invite them to learn how to throw a woman up against the wall, while bringing her their passionate energy and intensity. We practice this with our male clients and, if they have partners, we show them how to do it and they practice on their partners. If you have a partner, practice with her. If you don't and you are feeling brave, you can try this one on a date. You can also ask a friend if they will practice with you and give you feedback. Before you begin this exercise, you might want to do a session of Erotic Power Breath to get you in the mood. During this breathwork session, you can explore a fantasy of what passion looks like to you. This helps bring you to a state of grounded, centered arousal, which is the best state from which to do this exercise.

1. Have your practice partner stand with her back against the wall facing you, with you standing about four feet in front of her facing her.

2. When you feel ready, have her take a step towards you like she is greeting you or casually approaching you.

3. Look at her with all of your passionate intensity and push her back up against the wall, keeping eye contact. Throughout the whole experience, return to passionate eye contact with your partner. Feel free to look away to

admire the rest of her body or smell her neck, just make sure you come back to her eyes. With the eye contact, give her enough room between your face and hers that she can really see you. Do not kiss her, but instead, hold the sexual tension of the look. This builds anticipation in the body, which is often lost, especially in long-term relationships.

4. Even if she squirms, giggles or doesn't know how to receive it, do not back down. Stay there with her in a relaxed state, looking in her eyes and keeping connected with your passion and desire.

5. With one hand, hold her *tightly* around her waist. Hold her tightly enough that if she were to faint, you would be able to support her weight.

6. With the other hand, caress her face, her sides, her hips.

7. Play with variations of holding and caressing. For example, grab her ass tightly with one hand, lean in and smell her neck. Pin both arms above her head with one hand and gently caress her waist and hips. Spread her legs open with your knee and press your body closer to hers.

8. If you are doing it with a long-term partner or a friend, get some feedback about how it felt and try it a few times. You will be surprised at how powerful it can be with some additional information about what your partner wants and some practice.

Drive
Women Wild

Understanding & Satisfying Women's Desires

Women are highly sexual beings. To bring this out, you need tools that will please and seduce women across the spectrum, from women who are open and comfortable with their sexuality to women who are more shy or distanced from their desire. At this point, your work is half done because you are now bringing presence, acceptance, confidence, generosity and passion. You are in a place where the fun can really begin and grow. You will learn to have empathy both emotionally and sexually, curiosity and spontaneity in and out of the bedroom, and a sensual approach to life and sex.

In this section we give you the practical tools you need to understand women emotionally and sexually. You learn about women's bodies, desires, fantasies, and fears and how you can support them in opening up to their own sexuality and to you. When you are sexually confident, you create a space where she can explore her full potential. At the same time, many women are very shut down around their sexuality and may need to go on their own personal journey to open up; you can only support them, you can't take this journey for them or make them go on it. If you are with a woman who is shut down sexually, you can continue to feel your full sexual desire and invite her to take her own sexual journey. We help women with this all the time and our next book will be a map for women on how to connect with their sexuality and with men.

For this journey, you need to buckle up for a second and consider two questions: "Why women?" and "Why love?"

Why Women?

We know this might seem like a no-brainer because, if you are a heterosexual, you have no other choice, but we still think it is important for you to ask yourself, "Why women?" In this society everyone is assumed to be on the same trajectory, one which begins with an assumption of heterosexuality and moves on to attraction to the opposite sex, (maybe playing the field for a while), and meeting the right woman. Then, according to Hollywood, fairy tales and parental pressure, the trajectory is supposed to culminate with cohabitation, marriage and children. Because all of these steps are assumed, you may never have actually asked yourself, "Why would I want to have sex, intimacy and/or relationships with women?" It is a worthwhile exercise to take a moment and write a list of what you get out of engaging in intimate and sexual relationships with women. In other words, "Why bother?" Why would you want to spend the time, energy and effort it takes to make and maintain connections with women?

For each person, the answer is different, and we feel it might be helpful here to offer some ideas about what kinds of gifts women can offer you. At the most basic, embodied level, having great sex with a woman who you are attracted to gives you a feeling of power, self-connection, self-confidence and inner peace. Women can also help you to expand your emotional bandwidth; if you are open to growth, being with women can help you feel and process your emotions more deeply. While both men and women are, at birth, inherently emotional creatures, women are generally allowed much wider expression, and their ability to share these emotions can be a doorway into your own emotional connection with yourself. Women can bring you to the heights of your own passion, joy, fulfillment and inspiration.

While it is magnificent to soar on the wings of the sensual, emotional and inspirational experiences that women offer, this is not the only gift women bring to you as a man. In addition, they elicit many challenging emotions that lead you to your own personal growth. In relationships with women, you might feel confused, overwhelmed, afraid, anxious, rejected or angry and you may think to yourself, "Why would I want to put myself through all of these uncomfortable feelings?" Being in relationship with a woman gives you the opportunity to face and get comfortable with these emotions instead of feeling out of control and reacting to them. When you face these feelings triumphantly without hiding or apologizing, you realize that your freedom and power are solid.

Facing a partner is like looking in a mirror: you can hide or you can really allow yourself to show up from a place of openness with all of the excitement and fear right there. If you fully engage in this way, you can learn and grow into the strongest, most self-aware person you can be. By showing up fully as who you are, you find out if a woman is truly the right partner for you. If she is the right partner, you have the opportunity to feel deeply seen and acknowledged and find a greater acceptance for yourself. Finally, if you learn how to engage in relationships from a place of honesty and integrity, where you can love and accept both yourself and your partner, you find a sense of freedom you may never have experienced before.

Continuing your own growth and path while honestly engaging with your partner on an ongoing basis is the foundation for a lifetime of attraction to your partner. It is when we begin to stagnate or hide parts of ourselves that our sexual and intimate lives become routine and boring, but this is not inevitable. We have seen change in so many couples. Once they begin to open up and learn about each other in a new, fresh way, it is like starting a whole new honeymoon period.

Why Love?

Love is a deep surrender to your own emotions and desires, a release of your fears and an acceptance of yourself. It is actually a felt sensation in the body. Men and women have tremendous fears about this surrender. Men's greatest fear around love is that surrendering to love actually means that they have to surrender their personal freedom. Women's greatest fear about love is that surrendering to love leaves them open to loss if their man ceases to desire them.

Love is dependent on truth, integrity and communication. It takes a tremendous amount of bravery to tell the truth, to really ask for what you want, and to live in integrity. When you do this, you are ready to have and give the hottest sex because you are actually open to the possibility of love.

When you follow the steps in the first half of this

book and allow yourself to stay true to your sense of freedom and refuse to give away your personal power, you have the opportunity to experience real love. When you allow yourself to continue to grow and change and your lover to continue to grow and change, love stays fresh, and life stays engaging and inspiring.

Know the Playing Field

We have a tremendous amount of compassion for men in the face of what women expect of them. We work with women all the time helping them to get in touch with their own desires and to develop their own sexuality. We teach them to communicate clearly and openly what they need from men, and take responsibility for their own sense of self-worth and self-confidence.

At the same time, it is important for you to recognize that the current playing field is *not* full of women who feel confident and comfortable with their sexuality and there are many reasons for this. In this chapter we share some of the messages that women get around sex so that you can have compassion for women and know what to do when they are emoting.

You can begin to get a sense of women's sexuality from understanding what women consider their best sexual experiences. In order to contrast these experiences with most men's, we'll begin with two stories – one of a man's best sexual experience and the other, a woman's.

Jack's Story

"She showed up in this tight black mini-skirt and some kind of red top with sparkles on it so I knew she had sex on her mind. When we got back to my place I could tell it was on. As soon as we walked in the door, she started kissing me. It was so great to feel her so open and turned-on. That night, we must have done it in every room in the house. It started in the living room where she kneeled down in front of me and gave me head. I got so hard, I thought I was going to lose it. In the bedroom, I bent her over the side of the bed and she was so loud. She just kept coming and moaning and coming and the last time she squirted all over me. It was the first time any woman had ever done that. I swear I never came so hard in my life."

Janet's Story

We had just met the week before but I already knew he was the one. It was our third date and, up until then we had only kissed, but they had been the most passionate kisses of my life. At dinner, I could feel him wanting me, and the way he looked at me was so exciting. We went out dancing afterwards and he was so gentle, yet forceful. He pulled me close to him and I could feel his breath on my neck and his hands moving across my hips. I don't think we stayed very long. In the car on the way home, he was lightly

*stroking his hand up and down my leg and I could
feel myself starting to get excited, even though I rarely
got turned on that quickly. As soon as we walked in
the door we were kissing, even more passionately than
before. I just felt like he was there with me the whole
time, looking in my eyes when I went down on him.
He seemed to know exactly what to do. He picked me
up and carried me to the bedroom, set me down at the
side of the bed and gently pulled down my panties.
Then he grabbed my ass and pulled me toward him.
The forcefulness and gentleness made me crazy. I think
I must have come five times that night."*

Amazingly, these two stories are actually descriptions of the *same* experience. The stories come from a very effective exercise we do in our couple's workshop where both partners in the couple write about some sexual experience that they had together that they both thought was really hot. They have to decide on the experience together using only one sentence like "the time when we were at the hotel in Cancun" or, in the above case, "our third date." After that, they have to silently write out how they remember the experience. The stories by Jack and Janet are one of our favorites because you literally can't tell it is the same experience.

In our men's workshop, we offer a similar writing exercise to help men understand the difference between what they typically want and what women desire. We have men write about their best sexual experience and then we read some stories that women have written for us as well. As shown in Jack's story, we find that men's descriptions of their best sexual experiences are generally fast, hot, and to the point. They are usually very visual, genitally oriented and focus on sex acts. Often they take place in unusual locations like hotel elevators or include a surprise, like a friend who says, out of the blue, "I want you to rip off all of my clothes and fuck me right now." Many of them include women who initiate sex and are eager participants. They often also include descriptions of the women's pleasure, especially how many orgasms they have, how much they seem to want sex or how loud they are during sex.

Women's stories, like Janet's, are generally more drawn-out, with a storyline that begins well before any sex acts occur. They focus on desire, sensuality, passionate kisses and emotional connection. They contain men who range from confident to dominant, and who know how to take them sexually. They usually have longer descriptions of sensual seduction and foreplay. This is not to say that men don't like emotional, sensual sex or that woman don't like hot, to-the-point fucking; however, the consistency of differences in men's and women's stories does speak to what is most desirable for each. It also points to the way that men and women can find balance in their sexual relationships by communicating what is hottest for each of them.

The great news is that you can each have your best experience together. If you want your partner to be motivated to participate in the kinds of sexual experiences that interest you, it is essential to begin with curiosity and generosity in the face of her desires. Nothing makes a woman more ready, willing and excited about pleasing you as when she feels like you are curious about her desires and she has been extremely satisfied by the sex she is having with you. As you can see by the themes in women's hottest sexual stories, there are many aspects to what women want sexually. In order to take them to the heights of their sexual pleasure, you need to understand what they want and where these desires come from.

Understand Why Women Want What They Want

To understand what women want from their partners, you must understand how women were raised to think about sex and relationships. During their upbringing, women received very different messages about their sexuality than you did; these messages affect their sexual choices and self-image as well as their ability to communicate about and feel entitled to pleasure. Because of this, women rely on men's desire to help them feel their own arousal and desire. In fact, studies have shown that women don't even begin to feel sexual desire until they are already aroused.

When it Comes to Sex, Girls are Taught to "Just Say NO"

While boys' "birds and bees" talks focus on a gamut of topics including "playing the field," wet dreams and not getting girls pregnant, the talks that girls get focus almost exclusively on the perils of having sex. There is (almost) never any discussion of pleasure and "playing the field" for boys translates into being "easy" or a slut when it comes to girls.

Teachers and parents generally focus on teaching girls about reproduction, warn them about pregnancy and tell them that guys "only want one thing." Girls are responsible for keeping boys' sexual desires at bay in order to maintain their virginity and avoid pregnancy. Socially, they get messages about the dangers to their reputation. Having too much sex or liking it too much means that you are a slut.

Girls who enjoy sex and find themselves labeled as sluts might react in one of two ways: they can deny their enjoyment of sex or embrace it. Embracing it often re-sults in being sought out by boys for sex, but not for relationships and ridiculed by both boys and other girls. Being shunned by your peer group is one of the most primal, devastating feelings we can experience – humans and many social animals rely on this group quite literally for survival – and, for girls, being shunned and excluded as a "slut" touches on these primal fears, making them avoid it at all costs.

Another message that is heavily reinforced in popular literature, movies and television, is that girls and women are only valuable if they are in a relationship with a man. To get a man, they have to be outwardly sexy and attractive while, at the same time, needing to prove they are not sluts by withholding sex until they have gotten some sign of love or commitment. This puts girls and women in charge of being the gatekeepers around sex. To achieve this task, they have to shut down or distance from their own desires. As gatekeepers, it is no wonder that the most common sexual complaint among women is a lack of sexual desire. Ironically, girls and women are also supposed to dress and act provocatively, showing an external sexuality, while being disconnected from their internal desire, which can be very confusing to men.

Even those women who do have a clear idea of what makes their body feel the most pleasure rarely feel permission to explain this to their partners for many reasons. They often feel if they are too forward or aggressive about what they want, they may be seen as slutty, easy or unworthy of a relationship.

Women are Taught to Hate their Bodies

With so much pressure to look good, girls and women focus a tremendous amount of energy on being outwardly attractive as opposed to inwardly empowered.

They are much more highly prized if they are beautiful (based on the culture's current definition of beauty) while receiving terrible messages from the media, their families, friends and random strangers about their bodies. With this kind of policing, there is not a single woman in the U.S. who does not have some negative feeling about some part of her body.

Even women who appear to meet all of the cultural standards of beauty have body image issues. In fact, the women you think are the most physically attractive may have the worst body image problems because they are held and hold themselves to such a high standard. In a culture where women are valued for their beauty and desirability above all else, one of women's deepest desires is to feel beautiful and sexy to their partners all the time – this allows them to relax into their bodies and feel sexual without having to worry that they are constantly being judged on their appearance.

Good Girls Don't Ask for What They Want

In addition to distancing from their sexual desire, girls are also told to be "good" and "nice" and take care of others, and they worry that asking their partner to do something differently might hurt their partner's feelings. They fear it might be seen as unwomanly and jeopardize the relationship.

Girls and women are also told that true love means

that someone should automatically know what they want and how to please them. Many men buy into this idea as well. When we work directly with women, we explain that the idea that a partner should just know what she wants is a fairy tale. We point out that it is unlikely that a partner will know without any information or cues. The misleading cues, such as faked orgasms, that women sometimes give in order to try to make their partners feel good, exacerbate the problem since men don't even know when they aren't giving a woman what she needs. We also explain to women that telling a man what they want and then having him give it to them is a double gift – it means that he not only cares enough to listen, he also cares enough to follow through and try.

Women Are More Distractible From Their Sexual Feelings

In general, women are much more easily distractible from their sexual feelings than men. This means that it is easier for little interruptions to cause women's arousal to drop suddenly, and intrusive thoughts about responsibilities can come in and ruin the mood. People always want to know if this difference is biological or socially created. It is most likely a combination of both. Because of hormonal differences, women have a somewhat lower sex drive; however, as we explained, social messages make it hard for women to connect to their sexual selves.

Know the Way In

In the face of so many "no's" to sex, it is actually somewhat shocking that women experience sexual pleasure at all. Because women are not given a "yes" to sex, they rely on your desire and your ability to be the confident initiator of sex who takes them into their bodies and their arousal. The best ways into women's arousal are emotional connection and sensuality. Since women are raised as nurturers they are given more permission for touch and sensuality. Connecting to a woman's sensuality and having an understanding of how her body works can help you find the "yes" in her body instead of the "no" in her mind.

Most women allow themselves to experience the pleasure of sex only if it is in the context of a relationship or at least some form of emotional connection. This does not mean that you have to get into a relationship faster than you are comfortable with or ever, but it does mean that showing up from a place of honesty and emotional connection creates deeper comfort and openness. Some women do want just a casual experience, but this does not mean that they want a cold, distanced experience. They want the warmth and trust that comes from emotional connection no matter how long that connection lasts.

To help women to experience their full sexual potential, you need the personal sense of *Cockfidence* gained through the Qualities of presence, acceptance, confidence, generosity and passion as well as all of the Qualities to drive women wild, which include empathy, spontaneity, curiosity and sensuality.

Empathy

The key to getting in touch with a woman is through your own experience – we call it embodied empathy. Embodied empathy is the experience of being so connected with yourself and your internal sensations that you can feel your partner's emotions, bodily sensations, desires and responses in your own body. When you fully connect with your own body and hers, you have the ability to read her desires and follow both the verbal and non-verbal cues of her body such as shivers, breath (faster or slower), skin (i.e., goosebumps) and sounds (sighs or silence). The sentence that defines embodied empathy is, "I feel you."

Your ability to empathize has a huge bearing on your sex life, and particularly on whether you are going to get sex, how often, and how good the sex will be. When you tune into your own emotions by feeling the sensations in your body, you begin to feel when a woman desires you as well as what her body wants in sexual and intimate situations. Imagine your body is an antenna for her feelings – you can't be in her body, but you can listen to hers through your own.

To get in touch with your embodied empathy, pay attention to your sensations and emotions when you are around her. You can read so much of what is going on with her by your own reactions. When you read her like this, you can even try telling her what you are sensing inside of her, sometimes surprising her by pointing out emotions that she isn't even fully aware she is having. For example, you feel her excitement about an event in her life and say, "You look excited."

Embodied empathy also sensitizes your radar towards her more difficult emotions such as sadness and anger, allowing you to catch early warnings signs. This helps interrupt the escalation of drama and fights. With a little bit of practice, you can enhance your embodied empathy increasing your likelihood to have more great sex and less drama.

Connect Emotionally

Emotional connection, also known as "intimacy," is one of the most common desires that women have in relationship. And, while both men and women are deeply emotional creatures, men get very strong cultural messages about repressing their emotions. Women are generally given more permission for expression.

Take the same playground scenario we discussed in section one, where boys are told to buck up and stop crying. If a little girl were to get hit by a playmate her parents would generally pick her up with an, "Oh, sweetie, come here! Are you okay? Where does it hurt? Let me kiss it better," etc. These kinds of responses result in women staying more connected with and expressive of their emotions.

The differences in socialization around emotions often lead to a large difference in the amount of emotions women and men allow themselves to feel and express as well as the form in which they express them. Because men are taught to repress their emotions, they have less experience dealing with outward displays of emotion and are often overwhelmed in the face of a partner's tears or anger – particularly if they feel like they are responsible for the upset.

Women are much less likely to separate emotions into "positive" and "negative" the way that men do, which is why women might talk about having a "good cry," a phrase which may sound to you like an oxymoron. Women generally have a feeling of release or being cleaned out and opened up when they are able to express their emotions, especially when they feel seen, heard and understood. Emotions are not a problem to be fixed and the fact that a woman you are with has emotions does not mean that she is broken nor does it mean that you did something wrong.

Emotions are a doorway to deeper intimacy and trust. When emotions do bubble up, it is often a sign that a woman's feelings for you are deepening. The fact that she feels safe enough to let them out is a sign that she trusts that you can handle her. Each time your partner is upset it is actually an opportunity for you to feel confident, for her to feel listened to and for the two of you to get closer.

The payoff is that a woman who has released her feelings of frustration or resentment and who has been listened to often moves to a space of softness and receptivity in her body. When she lets out the emotional blocks in her body, she is more able to fully let you in and to allow her sexual energy to move freely in her own body and between the two of you.

In this section, we explain how to be with a woman when she is expressing her emotions. This is one of the most important skills you need to increase your ability to have better sex and close relationships with women. Once you realize what you need to do, you may find that, up until now, you have been doing *way too much*. Dealing with woman's emotions is simple but not necessarily easy.

A lot of men feel very confused by their partner; a guy will be going along in a relationship thinking everything is fine and then all of his partner's emotions burst out and it seems like everything is wrong. This happens because, even though girls are given more permission to express emotions, they are also told to be "good" or "nice" or take care of other people. As a result, women who feel that their emotions might overwhelm their partners let feelings build up and keep them stuffed inside.

When women are struggling constantly to try to make themselves less emotional, they become very small because their emotions are a great source of their power. Then men look at them and say, "Wow, I was so attracted to her when I first met her, she seemed so strong and like she knew what she wanted and now she is totally closed and distant and always trying to make everything okay." If you are attracted to feminine power and all of the sexuality and desire that implies, then learning how to engage with a woman's emotions is essential to your long-term happiness and attraction to your partner.

What women (and men) need around their emotions is to be heard and acknowledged. Ultimately, it is wonderful if a woman can tell you what her needs and feelings are as they are coming up in an open way. Some women are more capable of this than others and the way that you can help your partner is by valuing her emotions in a way that most of society do not. This is where empathy comes in – valuing a woman's emotions can be as deep as feeling her emotions with her, or it can happen by at least acknowledging them. A *Cockfident* man

"Are You On Your Period?"

This is a question you should *never* ask a woman when she is upset with you – she sees it as code for "You are being irrational and crazy and you should shut up." Because logic and reason are more highly valued in this society, when women communicate their needs and feelings from their emotions instead of laying them out logically and reasonably, they are accused of being hormonal or crazy. This makes it easy for men to dismiss women as irrational and to ignore the content of what they are saying. The messages girls get about being nice cause them to take care of others' needs and feelings before their own. Thus, they spend a lot of the month overlooking ways that they felt hurt or mistreated. At some point the feelings either erupt or lead to depression and erotic shutdown. Luckily, once a month, a woman's body goes through a hormonal surge that often lowers her tolerance for stuffing her emotions and, sometimes, even against her own will, these emotions come flooding out (also known as "PMS"). This is a great opportunity to practice all the skills you learn here and gain trust, intimacy and a deepened sexual connection with your partner.

doesn't say "Don't be sad right now," he validates her feeling by saying, "You're sad right now" or "I can feel how sad that makes you." When women feel their emotions are valid, they begin to listen to their emotions as one source of information and guidance and they can be in touch with the wisdom of their emotions instead of building up resentment, depression or rage. This wisdom can be used to move relationships into places of better communication, passion, intensity and intimacy.

Picture this: You are sitting at your favorite restaurant having a delicious dinner and a nice glass of wine. You remember your sweetheart was supposed to meet with her boss that day and you say, "So, what happened in your meeting today? Did you get that raise?" Suddenly, seemingly out of nowhere, she bursts into tears and says, "You don't think that I earn enough money!" You are thinking you were trying to be nice and you wonder where the hell the tears are coming from. Everything you say from there to console her seems to be digging the hole deeper. When your partner seems to be "over reacting," this is a sign that you have stepped on a land mine. There is something deeper here that she needs to share in order to be fully seen. Here is a moment for empathy – realizing what this is about for her, and not making it about you.

Many men, in these moments, feel like their partner is accusing them of doing something wrong. While it feels like you are being accused of being insensitive or critical, most of the time, you have done nothing wrong or you have made a small mistake that gets a big reaction.

When you think someone is attacking your abilities,

it can be devastating to your sense of self. You might feel as if being a good partner to a woman means knowing how to make her happy and to fix any problem so you become defensive. Because of this, most men never *really* listen to their partner in a way that makes her feel heard and helps her find her own truth or solution to their problem. Your job is not to fix. Believe us, the process of listening empathetically takes practice; you won't be perfect at it right away.

If you have never really listened to your partner, then you may need to listen to her for a while before she stops having outbursts all the time. On the other hand, if you have really listened, heard and understood all her underlying feelings and she comes at you over and over again with anger and resentment, she may need to do some therapeutic work for herself and you may need to evaluate your boundaries and clarify what you are willing to accept. Also, even if you are the best listener in the world, you *never* get rid of all of the painful emotions in a relationship, and that shouldn't be your goal. Life has challenges and its normal for relationships to have ups and downs.

Why It Feels So Hard

When you first hear a woman saying that you are doing something wrong or something that hurts her, you may feel criticized and begin to shut down, defend or distance. In order to protect themselves from these feelings, men take a number of actions, none of which actually allows a woman to release her emotions.

Defending and distancing are analogous to the instinctual responses of fight or flight. These instinctual responses are not happening because your life is literally threatened; they are happening because your sense of yourself as a good partner is threatened. When you are in one of these responses, you often fall back on old tools, such as pulling away, arguing or apologizing, which keep you from intimacy instead of helping you to cultivate it. As you read the list of the common defensive pitfalls, you may feel regretful of ways you have handled fights in the past. Try not to beat yourself up; there is little or no role-modeling for healthy communication in our society and plenty of role-modeling for the opposite – for a great example of what *not* to do, check out just about any reality television show.

The following is a list of common defensive pitfalls broken into "fight" and "flight" responses. The "fight" response generally looks like taking an action to change her feelings or shut them down:

1. **Debating** – Arguing with what she is saying to disprove her points, which makes her feel like she is wrong.

2. **Reasoning** – Trying to understand and logically explain what is happening in a calm, rational way, which often makes her feel like her feelings are irrational.

3. **Attacking** – Returning her accusations with your own, telling her all of the things she does wrong in the relationship. This makes her feel like she has to take care of you instead of allowing her to be heard.

4. **Fixing** – Jumping to the problem solving before getting down to what the real problem is, thinking that you are supposed to fix her feelings or her problems for her. This makes her feel like she is a problem to be solved instead of a human being to be seen and loved.

Flight generally looks like:

1. **Emotionally Leaving** – Leaving the connection (imagine that "blank stare") while sitting there and taking it. This makes her feel all alone.

2. **Physically Leaving** – Telling her you will talk with her later when she is less emotional and actually physically leaving the room or asking her to leave. This makes her feel patronized, rejected and unimportant.

3. **Appeasing** – Apologizing or agreeing with everything she is saying even if you aren't sorry or don't agree and trying to make everything okay even before you really know what is wrong. This makes your partner feel like you are weak, childish or disinterested in her real feelings and like she has to take care of you.

All of these are attempts to survive her emotions or make them go away without engaging with her or discovering the source of her sadness or anger. When you succumb to your defensiveness or your fears, then you have missed an amazing opportunity to help a woman deeply trust you and feel more intimacy with you. Deep inside, women are terrified that their emotions are too much for men to handle so women try to shut down their emotions to protect men. When all of a woman's energy is being utilized to contain and put away her own emotions, she is much less likely to fully open herself to you sexually. If you can handle all of her outside of the bedroom, she feels more free to bring all of herself to her sexual relationship with you as well.

Here are a few examples of common, defensive conversations. Before you read them we want you to know that you may see yourself in some of these examples and we don't want you to beat yourself up. It is rare to see good emotional communication modeled in our lives and pretty much everyone makes these mistakes all the time. While you read it, bring compassion to yourself and check your tendencies so you know your own pitfalls. You can also practice empathy by imagining yourself as the woman in the experience.

Todd and Janet had been together for nine months. In our initial separate sessions, Janet reported that she had pretty much lost her sex drive and Todd told me that he wanted to spice up their sex life. Twenty minutes into the first couple's session, they were talking about sushi.

Common Defensive Conversations:

#1

Janet: "I had been saying that I wanted sushi for the last week, but again last night we ended up at a steakhouse. I know sushi isn't your favorite food, but at least every once in a while we could go where I want."

Todd: "I'm sorry, we should go to sushi more often."*(appeasing)*

Janet: "I don't want you to just go along with everything that I say!"

#2

Janet: "You know what, I don't give a shit about sushi. I feel like you take me for granted, I have been trying to do all of these things to make you happy and you never even tell me you like them."

Todd: "What are you talking about? I give you compliments all the time! I just told you how great you looked in that dress before we left for dinner!"*(debating)*

Janet: Angry silence

Todd: "What? What did I do now?"

#3

Janet: "You don't care about what I want at all,

you only care about yourself!"

Todd: "Me? What about you? Everything I do, I do to make our life together better and all you are worried about is what you want all the time!"(attacking)

Janet: "Can you listen to me just once without telling me how awful I am?"

As you can see, none of these responses got Todd where he was trying to go. Conversations like these generally end with two people turned opposite directions in bed, angry or sad, and unable to sleep or move on from these negative feelings. Below, we have included the steps you can take to create a different kind of conversation, one that is not about who is right or wrong, or the facts, but about excavation – actually digging in deeper to get to the emotions that are underlying any conflict.

We are not saying that these emotional conversations are easy to navigate. The task of staying with the feelings and listening to accusations can be daunting and the fact that sometimes women seem to wind all over the place before getting to the point can be very confusing. It is possible to navigate through your partner's emotions, get to the deeper issues, help her release what she is holding, share your own feelings and come into deeper connection. Remember, this section is about empathy because empathy can make this process less daunting. When you keep an empathetic stance, you can feel what she is experiencing without defending yourself or trying to talk her out of it.

To help you navigate the excavation of your partner's underlying emotions, we have broken the process down into simple steps so that you can be a strong, non-defensive and empathetic listener to help her with this process. This is actually one of the qualities that women want in their partners more than anything else. Before learning the steps there are two things you need to know: firstly, it is not your job to make your partner happy and, secondly, it is impossible to avoid hurting your partner.

Realize it is Not Your Job to Make Your Partner Happy

The first thing to do is to quit the job you think you have, namely the job of making your partner happy. You can't. No one can make another person happy; you can only make yourself happy by being true to yourself, and giving in the ways you feel comfortable giving. If you try to be someone else to make your partner happy, or give up something essential to who you are, eventually you have to change back or leave in order feel like yourself again. We are not saying you should be a jerk. What we are saying is that, as long as you are actually taking the time to listen to and empathize with her feelings; are being honest with her; and are not being physically, verbally, emotionally or financially abusive, you are not making her unhappy. She might choose to stay in a relationship where she is not happy, but that is her choice and it is not your job to save her from herself.

When your partner has a strong reaction to something you say or do, you can bet that you are reminding her of painful experiences from her life, especially her childhood. *This is also true for you.* The problem is, in relationships, we take all of our partner's reactions to us very personally. So remember, even if she is upset about something you have done, your job is not to apologize or try to fix what she is saying you have done. Instead, it is the time to be *present* for her emotions, realize it is not about you and that there is a deeper wound there that you can let her feel and feel with her.

Realize it is Impossible to Avoid Hurting Your Partner

Because of fear of conflict, usually based on negative past experiences with conflict, some people try to live out entire relationships without ever hurting their partner or experiencing "difficult emotions" such as anger, frustration or sadness. However, since everyone has triggers, if you are going to be truly intimate with someone, you will press their buttons *no matter what you do*.

If you try to avoid pressing any buttons or run away from the emotions that emit when you do press one, you may momentarily avoid conflict, but you actually avoid intimacy. Each time you avoid conflict and run away from your partner's emotions, she is left filled with all these emotions. Her emotions fill her body like a balloon and we guarantee at some point she will either burst and stop feeling love for you, or float away and find someone else who can receive her emotions.

Instead of avoiding, begin to learn the signs that the balloon is filling up; that way you can elicit her emotions and deal with them before they get huge and out of control. This may seem like asking for trouble in the short-term, but ignoring them and letting them build creates a much worse situation in the long-term. You can tell when she is beginning to get upset by the tightness in her body, the tone of her voice, or a snappy or sarcastic response to something you say. That's the time to begin the process and interrupt the build-up, with a sentence like, "I know you just said you were fine, but it seems like there is some anger/frustration/sadness in your voice. Do you want to tell me what's up?"

Note: When women are in the highest states of sadness, fear or anger, they won't be able to process any information and trying to elicit information might even make things worse. They just need to be held or given some space and told simple, straightforward messages like, "I'm here with you" or "I love you" or "I'm not going anywhere." It is better to avoid phrases like, "Shhhhhh, it's going to be okay," because these make her feel like she has to calm down to make you feel better.

If you follow these 9 steps, you can resolve almost anything:

1. Breathe and come into presence

Use the Sexual Embodiment Breath to find a place of physical relaxation that is coming from deep in your body (not your mind). Be gentle with yourself through this process. There may be some wonderful things for you to learn about yourself from what she is saying, but don't get caught up in this being about you. If you happen to get defensive you can get back on track by coming back into presence.

It is never too late and a great tool can be the "Do Over." This is when you realize you have gone down one of the unhelpful pathways (arguing, attacking, etc.) and you can say, "Wait a minute, I realize I was arguing with what you were saying without even hearing it yet. Can we try that again?"

2. Remember that you have time

In moments like these that are full of adrenaline and anxiety, you actually have much more time than you think you do. There is no urgency for you to explain yourself, answer any of her accusations, or solve anything. It is okay to go slowly so that you can understand what is actually going on underneath all the words that are coming out.

3. Understand that her emotions are an offering of trust

When you see your partner is upset, remind yourself that her emotions are a compliment and not a condemnation of you. When she brings them to you it is a sign that she believes in you and trusts you can be there with her. As we noted above, many women feel that they are too emotional or too much for their partners so they hold these parts of themselves inside. If she is bringing them out, it means she believes that you can handle all of her. When she can trust that you aren't going anywhere when she is hurting, she is also more likely to open to you sexually when things are going better (and if you follow these steps, things may be going better in twenty minutes).

4. Don't act on your impulse to defend yourself

Relationships never become more intimate by figuring out who is "right" and "wrong," but conversations often end up in these kind of defensive debates. Defensiveness is an extremely important reaction to notice. It might mean part of you agrees with what she's saying or it might mean you are afraid of losing the argument or that you are agreeing to give in to whatever she wants. If you listen to her feelings, that doesn't mean you are agreeing to do anything or be anything different in the relationship.

Instead of getting defensive, we suggest you simply realize your partner is having feelings right now and she needs to express them. This is not about you being a bad person and it doesn't mean that you are in a bad relationship, it is just about her needing to get her feelings out.

When you do this, a woman feels acknowledged and can really open up and trust in you.

5. Put yourself in her shoes

Empathy is a simple desire to want to know and understand your partner more deeply. Empathy is actually putting yourself in another persons shoes and imagining what it would be like to have the experience they are having. Some men avoid this because they think that really understanding how their partner is feeling will mean that they are "wrong" or that they need to stop doing something that is really important to them. It is essential to differentiate between understanding something and trying to fix it. Just because she is hurt by something you did, doesn't mean that you did something wrong or that you need to change. It is not about whether her feelings are justified or "true" or "false" or "right" or "wrong" yet many men and women get caught up in true/false, right/wrong conversations, which never creates deeper intimacy. By empathizing with what your partner is feeling without making it right or wrong or changing yourself in the face of her feelings, you offer her space to be exactly who she is and for you to stay who you are in that moment instead of wishing she were having some other reaction.

6. Listen for and speak to the underlying emotions (not the criticism)

When women feel something, the words may come

out as a big jumble of accusations, interrogations or criticisms and you might not even know what she is trying to tell you. If what you are hearing is criticism, you haven't gotten to the underlying feeling or emotion that she is trying to get across. Criticism is like static on a radio: until you find a way to tune into what is actually going on, you are not getting any of the important content. When she says something like, "You never call me" or "You care more about what's on television than me," what is underneath is almost always a feeling like, "I feel lonely," "I feel like you don't love me," "I feel like you don't want me," "I feel undesirable."

So you are probably thinking to yourself, "Why don't women tell me what they are feeling or ask for what they need instead of building up resentment and criticizing?" In a perfect world, we would all learn that we can ask for what we want directly. Unfortunately, that is not the training that most women have had. Again, because women are told to be nice and often fear being left if they really assert their needs and desires, they avoid being up front and direct.

You can help by listening to what she is saying and trying to help her identify the underlying feeling. If strong emotions are coming up, the content (money, sex or who was supposed to take out the garbage) is not important. *What is being worked on is your emotional connection with your partner.* Emotional conversations are never about what they seem to be about; they are about underlying feelings and fears like loneliness, lovability, desirability, or feeling important.

If she says something like, "You never appreciate anything that I do," you could say something defensive like, "I just told you yesterday how much easier you make my life," which will probably shut her down or make her feel like she is crazy. Or, you could say something like, "It seems like you feel like you are not important." Or, you have just come back from a business trip and she says something like, "At work I have to do everything by myself and then you are gone and I only hear from you every three days and you barely have time to talk." You might respond condescendingly with "You know I have to work constantly on those trips and I don't get a moment to myself." Or you could say, "It sounds like you might feel really alone."

When listening, if she shares a feeling word, it is actually most effective to repeat the exact key word and not a synonym. If she says, "I'm really angry that you didn't drop off the mail," you can say, "It sounds like you are really angry." If there is no feeling word there, just take a guess then listen carefully and let her tell you what she is feeling. She will usually tell you if you got it right or she will correct you. If she doesn't correct you but her body doesn't relax or she physically pulls back, you have probably missed the mark. Acknowledge that you didn't get it right and ask her for guidance. Once you get it right, allow yourself to celebrate the moment of empathy – it means you have worked together to more deeply understand what she is feeling.

An emotionally empathetic response diffuses anger and allows her to feel closer to you again. If done on an ongoing basis, she is likely to move quickly from accusations to empathy for you, and may even be able to volunteer the emotion she is having before you need to dig.

A note about crying: Some men don't realize that crying is actually a step in the *right* direction. When a woman comes to you full of frustration or anger and appears tense and rigid, she may not seem that emotional. However, you will hear emotion in her tone or read it in the clenched way she is holding her body. Once she feels you understand what she is saying, she might begin to cry. Many men at this moment feel they have done something wrong or made it worse, but crying (or actually feeling their emotions in some way) is what women (and men) need to experience in order to feel good and calm again in their bodies. Crying can be the release of air from the balloon; it often happens when your partner feels that you actually care about and want to understand her.

7. Establish supportive physical touch

We put this near the end because she might not be ready for touch right away but, as soon as you see some softening in her body towards you, you might try taking her hand, putting a hand on her leg or perhaps holding her in your arms. Go slow with touch and notice if she softens more or tenses more. If she softens, keep the connection. Studies have shown that couples' nervous systems (like parents' and children's nervous systems) become intertwined and start co-regulating with one another. In other words, the more tense you are, the more tense she will be, the calmer you are, the calmer she will be. If you can stay grounded, relaxed and present, physical connection can increase co-regulation and help to bring your partner into a more relaxed, grounded state herself.

Connecting through touch also shows her that you want to be connected with her and displays a great amount of confidence as long as you are feeling ready to touch her. Especially if she is so upset that she doesn't have words for her feelings in the moment, hold her close and remind her that you are there with her and that you love her or care deeply about her.

8. Reassure

Once you really understand the underlying feelings, there is likely nothing left to do. If it feels appropriate at this moment, you might give her some reassuring words such as, "I didn't realize that when I didn't call for a few days, you felt so lonely or uncared for; it is never my intention to make you feel this way." *Do not* jump the gun on reassurance. By the time you are reassuring, her breath should be relaxed and her body soft, and she should already feel like you understand what was going on for her.

Let's return to Todd and Janet.

Janet: "I had been saying that I wanted sushi for the last week, but again last night we ended up a steakhouse. I know sushi isn't your favorite food, but at least every once in a while we could go where I want."

Todd: "It sounds like you are feeling taken for granted and maybe you are a bit frustrated with me."

Janet: "No, not really frustrated. It's more like you're not taking me seriously."

Todd: "Okay, can you tell me more about how you feel I'm not taking you seriously?" Janet: (starts to cry): "It's just, it's just, well, we have been together for nine months and we still haven't talked at all about the future."

Todd: "So you have been thinking about our future together and you feel alone in that, like you are the only one thinking about it."

Janet: "Yes!" Janet's body begins to visibly soften as she allows herself to be vulnerable and honest about what had been going on.

Todd: "I see now that you have been feeling like our relationship is not as important to me as it is to you and I never want you to feel that way."

It seems bewildering right? How on earth did Janet get from angry about sushi to upset that they had not been talking about the future. Todd and Janet were actually clients of ours and, once we went deeply into the conversation we found out where all this had come from. Over the last two weeks, it seemed that everyone Todd and Janet socialized with was talking about how in love they were with their partners. Every couple around them seemed to be planning on moving in or talking marriage and babies. Janet had realized that the future never came up when she talked with Todd and pretty soon she was obsessing about it. For many reasons, including the worry that Todd would be frightened at the thought of talking about the future, she had decided against bringing up.

The problem was that these feelings were bubbling under the surface and, for whatever reason, the steakhouse the night before had been the final straw – she couldn't hold it any longer. She felt that Todd must not really love or want her since he had never talked about what might happen next in their relationship. If Todd and Janet had stayed with the sushi conversation or debated whether or not he was taking her for granted, he never would have heard what the real issue was or how she was really feeling.

9. Share your feelings

Once your partner feels relaxed, connected to you,

heard and seen, she may be ready to hear about your feelings and thoughts. When you share make sure you dig for your underlying feelings as well and don't go into facts or logic. She can only empathize with you if she knows what is going on in your emotional world. When you share your feelings and thoughts you may hit a few more buttons and bring up new feelings for her so be prepared to loop through some of the steps multiple times in a single conversation; however, if you keep with the steps, it is more likely that these conversations will become less painful and you will both get back to relaxed comfort more quickly each time.

Here is how Todd shared his emotions with Janet:

Todd: "This relationship is important for me and, at the same time, in past relationships I have felt pushed to move in quickly. This is probably why I have been avoiding the conversation. I'm realizing that in relationships, I often worry that I need more alone time than my partner wants me to have and I always feel like I need to give up on my alone time to make her happy."

Janet: "Well you can have as much alone time as you need."

Todd: "I know that that's what you feel, but it isn't about you giving me space it is about me trusting my-self to protect my personal time and needs. I want to continue to grow this relationship with you and, now that you have expressed that it is important for you to move in, I would love to keep the conversation going about moving in and how I can keep my personal time."

Note that Todd did not give Janet an answer right away; her desire to move in had come as news to him and he needed time to feel his own feelings about them moving in together.

When sharing your feelings, make sure you give yourself time to actually feel before you make any decisions. At the same time, don't put off the conversation indefinitely, as it will continue to boil under the surface if it is not addressed.

Be Vulnerable, not Weak

As men, you are given the message throughout your life that showing how you feel or asking for support means that you are weak. It is extremely important to distinguish between weakness and vulnerability. Vulnerability is strong; neediness is weak. Neediness is when you share something with a partner with the expectation that she is supposed to make it better or take care of you. Ultimately, in the same way that a woman's feelings are hers and not yours to fix, your feelings are yours and it is your responsibility to work through them.

At the same time, talking to your partner about your fears or hurts allows her into a part of you that most of the world doesn't usually see. You will be surprised at how much showing your vulnerability without being needy will turn your partner on. Women want strong men. Being vulnerable is one of the strongest things you can do because it shows your humanness and invites her to connect to her own humanness and vulnerability. When you are vulnerable about your feelings or fears, it means you are both safe to be imperfect and to trust that you can still be loved in the midst of this imperfection. In short, vulnerability is hot and the hottest sex for women often comes after deep, emotional sharing takes place.

Get Turned On By Her Turn On

Once she feels your emotional empathy, the next step is to have sexual empathy. Unless you have actually experienced it, getting turned on by your partner's turn-on is a concept that may feel foreign to you. Often when men and women have sex together, it is a goal-oriented experience of turn-taking, where each one of you is focused on giving the other person an orgasm and achieving your own orgasm, with very little connection or energetic reciprocity.

We call the rush to orgasm "work mode" because it feels like each of you is trying as quickly as possible to get to your orgasm, often losing touch with your partner. Work mode robs you and your partner from reaching the heights of your sexual potential. Women's sexuality is endless and they can have many orgasms in one encounter. When you are able to channel her sexual pleasure through your body, it increases your potential for sexual sensation exponentially. Men can learn to be endless in the same way as women. By connecting with your own body and tuning into hers, you begin to feel the waves of her arousal move through your body (see the exercise at the end of this chapter).

Read Her Non-Verbal Cues

If you are with a woman who is communicative and who has really learned about her body, she can tell you a lot about how she wants to be touched and where. However, many women do not learn a lot about their bodies and desires and feel shy asking for what they want. Even a woman who sometimes knows exactly what she wants may not always know and wants you to bring new ideas and creativity. Whether or not your partner is someone who is able to communicate her desires to you, it is also essential that you be able to read a woman's non-verbal cues.

To read her non-verbal cues, you need to tune into your own body with presence and empathy, allowing your body to feel her turn on, and using your senses to read what is going on her body. There are many cues you can read from your partner's body that communicate what she likes and how turned on she is at any particular moment. You can use all five of your senses to read these cues. This is a great time to add that sex is messy and, if you want to really enjoy all that it has to offer, you have to be willing to dive in, get wet, smell, savor and connect with all your senses.

Sight – Watch for the following bodily changes that indicate arousal. She may experience flushing where her face or other parts of her body, most often her chest or neck, get red and splotchy. Her pupils dilate and her lips become fuller. Her nipples may also increase in size and become erect and she may get goose bumps. In addition, her body's movements indicate arousal. Arching her back or moving her pelvis are indicators of arousal, while putting her ass in the air may mean that she wants more touch on her ass.

Sound – Listen for changes in her breathing. Deepening of breath means she is relaxing, rapid breathing indicates heightened arousal as does an increase in her heart rate. Notice when she is moaning or making sounds of pleasure; these are important indicators of enjoyment that help you identify what works for her.

Smell – When a woman becomes aroused, she begins to release pheromones that change the scent of her body. The most significant changes can be detected in her armpits (sometimes even if she is wearing deodorant) and her pussy as she begins to lubricate. While some men are very distanced from their ability to read these scents, it can be extremely erotic for both you and your partner to dive into this sense of smell and allow the changes in scent to move through your own body and increase your arousal. You can do this by smelling her armpits or her pussy.

Taste – As pheromones are released, they can also be detected through taste. You can try licking her armpits and tasting her pussy as you sense the changes in smell to notice if you can sense the tastes changing as well. Again, see how much you can channel the sensual enjoyment of these changes through your own body.

Touch – In addition to the redness of flushing, you can also notice heat shifting in her body as the blood gets redirected into the face, nipples and genitals. Her checks, chest and pussy may become warmer to the touch and you can also feel for erect nipples and pussy lubrication. As she gets more aroused, she may also touch your body more; notice when she grabs for you or her grip on you tightens. In response to your touch, you may also feel goose bumps on her body. You may feel certain parts of her body move closer to your hands or mouth, meaning that those parts want touch or deeper touch; if she moves them away, those parts may be done with touch or want lighter touch.

EXERCISE
Create a Pleasure Circuit

You need a practice partner for this exercise. Lie together next to one another or sit face-to-face. Begin with your eyes closed and, together, do a session of Erotic Power Breath. Once you feel the erotic connection flowing from your pelvic floor through to the top of your head, channel the erotic energy into your hands and arms so that you feel your hands as an extension of your cock.

Take turns giving and receiving touch while keeping the circuit going with eye contact and synchronized breath. Start with giving touch for your own pleasure. Explore touching her body while focusing your attention on the pleasure that your hands derive from touching her skin. This allows you to connect with your embodied empathy and makes you a better giver – what feels good to you feels even better to her.

Continue to give touch to your partner's arms or hands from your own desire, staying connected with your erotic energy throughout the experience. As you continue to breathe, feel each breath connecting your erotic energy to the touch you are giving your partner. Allow your body to feel any arousal that comes from touching her and that comes from the arousal that you are giving her in her body. Notice her non-verbal cues such as goose bumps or flushing of the skin or ask her how she wants to be touched so that she can reach higher levels of arousal.

See if you can begin to ride the wave of her arousal by feeling the way that your cock is always internally connected to your hands. Let her arousal move up and down the center of your body. If you need an extra boost to help you stay more in touch with your cock, squeeze your PC muscles or rock your pelvis. By creating new neural pathways of pleasure in your body, this exercise sets the foundation for experiencing her arousal, pleasure and orgasm in your own body. When it is her turn to receive, in giving her pleasure, you are actually receiving pleasure as well. Let her then take a turn being the giver of touch and feel her arousal increase with your pleasure. Your pleasure in receiving increases her arousal. Throughout the experience of giving and receiving, together you are sharing a full pleasure circuit.

Curiosity

Curiosity is a state of non-judgmental openness and a desire to learn more about a person, to try new experiences, and to better understand yourself without judgment or an attachment to outcome. As a lover, it is shown by a willingness to continue to ask and listen to what a woman wants in any way or at any time she wants to tell you as well as a deep desire to understand exactly what makes her tick in the bedroom.

The sentence that defines curiosity is "I want to know you." Learning about sex, women, and intimacy is an ongoing process full of ups and downs. Reading this book shows that you already have a good dose of curiosity and taking this curiosity into your interactions with women can bring you quickly to places of deep attraction and connection.

When a man enters into an experience with a particular woman, he may attempt to avoid any perceived negative experiences and skirt around any challenges. This can result in his being controlling, outcome-driven, self-critical, judgmental or fearful. This approach hinders the natural flow of energy between two people, and makes it much more likely that an interaction ends up feeling difficult, stilted and unsatisfactory.

A much more comfortable place from which to approach women – and the world in general – is from a place of curiosity. Curiosity is a way of looking at each new experience from a receptive, open place, without judgment or any sense of what the outcome might be. You just feel an experience in the moment. Taking this approach gives you an opportunity to see what you can learn about yourself and the women in your life. Being an Extraordinary Lover means you are always discovering and having fun, hot, exciting sex – all of which require a healthy dose of curiosity.

This state of open curiosity need not only apply when you are connecting with a woman for the first time, but can be an ongoing approach. The beauty of curiosity is that it allows for the natural joys and challenges that happen over time between two people. An ongoing state of curiosity also acknowledges that you and the woman you are interacting with can and will change over time. So often in relationships a desire to control the unknown leads to stagnation and boredom. An attitude of curiosity joyfully invites the unknown, making room for ongoing growth, excitement and passion between you and your partner.

Part of being curious means being open to many possibilities. While we offer you information about women to help you better understand their different psychology and biology, make sure to stay curious about your partner's unique desires.

Know When She's Horny

You may already know that women are cyclical creatures. If the woman you are with is still menstruating, there is generally a time in her cycle when you are more careful, trying to avoid the mood changes that sometimes come along with hormonal changes. We call this time of the month premenstrual syndrome or PMS (see the sidebar "Are You on Your Period?" in Quality 6: Empathy). What many men don't realize is that there is also a time in a woman's cycle where she is much hornier and more easily aroused.

During puberty, girls have hormonal surges in much the same way that boys do, increasing their natural desire for sex. Unfortunately many social messages distance girls and women from this natural flow of desire. As women get a little bit older, generally somewhere in their mid- to late-twenties, their hormonal rush settles down and their level of sex hormones fluctuates greatly throughout their menstrual cycle. Desire changes for women when they leave the rushing hormonal phase in their teens and early twenties, when they are pregnant, after they give birth, or once they have gone through menopause.

To know when your partner is horny, it can be helpful for you to keep track of her menstrual cycle. Women who are still menstruating are generally most physiologically horny during ovulation (about 14 days before they begin to bleed) and right before or during menstruation. This does not mean that women do not want sex other times of the month; a woman can get horny through romance, fantasy, seductive touch or other cues aside from physiological horniness. However, it may serve you to know that she is much more likely to respond to your advances during ovulation and menstruation. She generally warms up more quickly, so she might be more likely to enjoy a quickie. These are also the times of the month when she has the most potential for sustained pleasure and multiple orgasms.

The rest of the month when women are not as hormonally motivated for sex, they need some external motivation to connect with their sexuality. Studies have shown that when women first get into a relationship they temporarily lose their hormonal cyclicity and are more consistently physiologically aroused throughout the month. Women are not being manipulative by having a lot of sex with you in the beginning of a relationship and then being less interested later on; they are simply following their hormones. After this honeymoon period women often need more warm-up or seduction to get their sexual energy fully engaged. *Studies have also shown that for many women, desire follows arousal – not the other way around as it is for men. In other words, until a woman starts to feel some kind of arousal in her body, sex is often not on her mind.*

Unfortunately, most of the romance and seduction in a relationship happens at the beginning. During this time, each person seems new and exciting and both partners are generally more anxious about whether or not the relationship will last. Once the relationship becomes more stable, women's sex hormones return to their natural cycle, and both men and women get lazy about seducing their partner. Sex often becomes routine, boring, less frequent or even non-existent. In order to keep sex exciting in long-term relationships, it is essential to begin to take a conscious approach to sexual connection instead of assuming it is just going to happen. The quality of maintaining curiosity, or allowing a feeling of change and newness, is a key to maintaining this excitement.

Understand Her Feelings About Her Body

In our society women receive messages that only one

type of body is attractive and sexy – this gets in the way of most women ever feeling completely sexy and comfortable with their bodies. Many women are waiting until they have the perfect body to allow themselves the pleasures of sex. For women who don't feel good about their bodies, chances are low that they fully embrace and enjoy their sexuality.

During sex, women often "spectate," meaning they are emotionally outside of their bodies looking at themselves with a critical eye for fat, cellulite or wrinkles. Positive body image is an important step to uninhibited and wild sexuality. Women get so many daily negative messages about their bodies and how a perfect body should look; they can use your help in combating them. One thing that helps women feel sexy and sexual is to feel how sexy and attractive you think she is.

When we talk about this to men, they often ask, "But what if I don't like her stomach?" or "what if I'm not that physically attracted to her?" One of the wonderful things about you getting connected with your own body and your erotic power is that attraction deepens when you are in your body and connected to your partner. It is possible to have attraction when you are disconnected from your body, however it is an objectified attraction based almost completely on the way a woman looks and not on the ways that you are connected. When you follow the steps in the first section of this book and are actually in your body and connected to your partner, you will find all of her attractive – this is what we call embodied attraction.

If you are really connected to yourself and you still don't feel attraction with a partner, it probably means that you are not really connecting and you may either need to do some work to learn to connect more deeply or you may need to find a partner to whom you feel more connected. On the other hand, if you are using the idea that you are not attracted to a woman over and over again to move from one woman to another, you may want to take a look at this pattern with some curiosity and see what fears are underlying it.

While it is not your job to fix a woman's body image issues, and it is wonderful if women take the time to consciously work through negative body image, one of the gifts that you can give your partner is to tell her on a regular basis how much you love her body and her appearance. Remember, women have a very long memory for criticism; she will remember the sentence "Your butt looks kinda big in those jeans" for the rest of her life. If, on the other hand, you love big butts, you might say, "Your butt looks so deliciously round in those jeans, I may have to take them right back off of you," then you are helping her see those curves in a different light.

Don't let women mislead you; when they ask, "how do I look?" they don't want to hear that their thighs are big, or that you like their hair longer, or their breasts perkier; they definitely don't want to see something less than enthusiastic admiration in your eyes. Make sure when you give a compliment that you are fully present and, if possible, giving her direct eye contact.

It is especially helpful if you happen to love parts of her body that she hates and you can sincerely show them love. You can do this both by telling her how amazing those parts of her are and giving them lots of physical affection, positive attention, and adoration like kisses and caresses – even grabbing if she likes it.

When we talk to men about body image, we often hear men say, "She knows I think she is beautiful; I told her that all the time when we first started going out," or "I just told her last month that she looked great in that outfit," or "I remember I told her she was beautiful at least once this week." If you have the urge to say any of these sentences, you are likely missing an essential part of understanding what makes your partner feel great. She needs to hear it *whenever it spontaneously comes into your mind.*

The more that you give women these positive messages about their bodies and how much you desire them, the more they want to be naked in front of you and the more that they feel comfortable being sexual with you. There are a few key body areas that receive the brunt of women's negative attention. They are stomachs, thighs, breasts, butts and pussies. When women look in the mirror, there is a voice inside her head saying, "My thighs are so fat," or "I hate my stomach."

You can be at least one interruption to this voice. Unfortunately, there are many voices that give her the opposite message including fashion magazines, movies, television, and clothing stores, so she may reject these messages at first or need them often. Even if she is hearing negative messages everywhere and saying them to herself, you can tell her how much you love her body and want it exactly the way that it is. Curiosity doesn't only mean that you want to get to know your partner – it also means to have curiosity within yourself and that you are open to what turns you on. When you are open and curious, genuine compliments come much more easily.

A female client once told us, "I will never forget the first man who told me that he loved my thighs. I was 26 and when he said it I thought he was crazy or joking, but when I saw the way that he looked at them, as though they were a sweet bowl of ice cream he couldn't wait to get a bite of, and the way that he caressed them and kissed them when we were making love, I knew he really meant it. It was the first time in my life I even considered that my thighs could be loveable. Now when I look in the mirror, it is like I see them through his eyes; I love their shape, their softness, the muscles." When asked how she felt about this partner, she said, "I was very grateful for him and also very turned on by him all the time because he looked at my body with such desire. You should have heard the sweet things he said about my pussy!"

Many women have negative feelings about their pussy. They are often told that this is a dirty part of their body that smells and tastes bad and these beliefs interrupt their connection to their own sensations and their enjoyment of receiving oral sex. So, if you love the way that your partner's pussy looks, smells and tastes, give her some of this feedback. Tell her how beautiful her pussy is or how delicious it tastes. By expressing your desire for her smell and flavor, she begins to feel more positive about her pussy.

Sometimes learning to pay compliments takes a fundamental shift in the way that you think because men often see the need or desire for compliments as a weakness. Whereas men pride themselves on achieving everything on their own, women give each other praise and support for accomplishments. When you give a woman more verbal support and reassurance (about how important they are, how beautiful they are, or how much you love them), you experience the payoff. You will see them grow more confident and powerful in their own feelings about themselves, which will make them sexier to you.

When giving compliments, the more specific and descriptive you can be, the better. For example, women may have heard "you look beautiful" thousands of times. It is not that she minds hearing it again, but you stand out in her mind if you can say something about her that you appreciate that she has heard much less frequently like, "The way your hair is falling in front of your eyes is so sexy, I feel like you are this mysterious woman who I can never know enough about."

You may look over at her sometimes and think, "God, she is hot" or "I really want to fuck her right now," and those are great thoughts and feelings to share with her, just remember to translate them into her seduction language (which we cover in Chapter 8).

Don't forget, women also want to be appreciated as a whole human being, so noticing all of your partner's amazing qualities and appreciating them verbally is highly valuable. Share your respect her for her intelligence, her talents, her interpersonal skills and her interests and you will likely feel this appreciation coming back your way as well.

Know How to Approach Her

As a result of being distanced from their desires and not feeling entitled to go out and get what they want sexually without feeling like a slut, women want men to "take them." The way to take a woman is by appealing to her body instead of her mind. Women want men to take charge and lead them into their sexuality so that they can enjoy the experience without having to think too much about it.

Women do not want to think about what they are doing sexually because the main messages they received about sex were to avoid it. *As much as society has tried to rob women of their sexuality, somewhere, in every woman's body, is a reservoir of desire and excitement waiting to find its flow.* It may be buried very deeply or may be much closer to the surface. Either way, if she allows herself to go there, amazing sex can happen. If you approach a woman with an understanding of how to take her there, you have the power to show her parts of herself she never knew existed. When you take charge, she opens herself and really lets you inside so you can experience a whole different level of sexual power and release.

We understand more than most people that you may be frustrated with women if they don't communicate about or initiate sex. We have a tremendous amount of sympathy for you because, whether you are doing it for the first time or the thousandth time, taking charge and knowing how to really speak to a woman's body takes a lot of confidence. Especially since you may have to sit with her through the times when her mind is saying "no" and not take her "no" as a rejection.

While we constantly teach women to get connected to their desire and to find out and ask for what they need around romance, seduction, and sensuality, it is also important for you to be realistic about the current playing field. Women are inexperienced with communicating their sexual desires and are uninformed regarding sexual techniques. When you ask them what they want, they may feel pulled into their head and, at a subconscious level, all the messages about not being allowed to be sexual may come rushing in. This may cause them to shut down, get turned off, or distance from their desires. Because of this, the women you encounter may be confusing, unclear or short with you, which is one of the reasons we have written a book for you, so that you can approach women in a way that helps you *and* them to find out what they truly want. *Sometimes for a woman to get into her sexuality it takes a man who can bring her there.*

Some men are sensitive to cues of rejection, and when presented with something from a woman that feels like rejection, they give up. Maybe they don't want to be disrespectful or cross a woman's boundaries, hurt anyone, or face a more direct rejection, so they simply back off. Unfortunately, part of what women have been taught around sexuality is that they are supposed to say "no" to sex and so the first responses from a woman around sex almost always look like a no. A man who has it all is a man who takes initiative, who appeals to a woman's body instead of her mind, who doesn't back down at any slight hint of rejection, but who still takes a woman's boundaries and desires seriously and stops when she is not wanting it. You may have already learned that asking "Do you want to have sex?" can bring her to her head and may not get you anywhere. Verbal or physical seduction usually gets far better results.

In the last year, Allen had had thirty first dates and three second dates, and he'd had sex with exactly one woman, once. According to him, "It wasn't that great." When we asked Allen how he approached the transition to sex he said, "I always feel awkward knowing that she expects me to make the first move, I get self-conscious and lose track of what I'm saying and what she is saying as I try to plan where to fit in the first kiss." As he talked, he shifted in his seat and the awkwardness and tension in his body was palpable. Then what? "Well, then I say something like, 'You're really beautiful, can I kiss you?'" Usually this ends in a half-hearted kiss, a hasty and excuse-filled goodbye and no returned phone calls."

Allen's problem was clear. He was uncomfortable being the initiator so he spent his entire time with women worrying about what to do next and appealing to her mind instead of her body. Women he was dating undoubtedly felt the lack of self-confidence that his body was communicating and, at the same time, they were pulled into their mind by his question. When they had to think about it, all of their "NOs" arose. These women were probably thinking, "Is it too early to kiss him? Will he think I'm easy?" Even if they wanted him moments before, were hoping and wishing he'd kiss them, the question, "Can I kiss you?" was enough to take the woman out of her desire and change her internal "yes" to a self-conscious "no."

In working with Allen, we began with getting him connected to his body through breath and other techniques we covered in the first section of this book.

As Allen began to practice presence and curiosity, he was able to stay connected. He began to build confidence in that connection and in his own desires and desirability. Most importantly, he began to realize that he already had an internal gauge that told him when women were opening to him. Instead of asking for permission, when he saw "the look" of receptivity and readiness in her eyes, he just moved in for a kiss. If she wasn't ready, he did not take it as a personal rejection and stayed present with her. "It was crazy! Staying connected with a woman when she wouldn't kiss me ended in hotter experiences than when a woman was ready to kiss me right away. This one woman actually seemed surprised and grateful that I didn't act all rejected. About 10 minutes later, she leaned over and started kissing me."

By staying present, Allen showed his solidity and confidence in himself, increasing his partner's trust in him and giving her time to get used to the idea of kiss-

*ing him. His continued presence even ended up in one
of men's favorite fantasies, a woman taking sexual
initiative. "The more I stayed present, the more she
came after me," he added with a satisfied smile on his
face, "She completely tore me apart that night."*

This same approach of staying present and reading cues can also help take you through the sexual "bases" with a woman. If you have kissed her and are ready to move further, you can continue to read her body language and pay attention to her body's boundaries, which shift throughout any sexual experience. Oftentimes women, before they even leave their house for a date, decide how far they are willing to go sexually that evening. Women make these decisions before they leave the house because they know they may not be able to trust themselves in the heat of the moment when their sexual desire takes over. We feel it is unfortunate that women think that they have to make these pre-date decisions because it means they are not letting themselves be true to what they actually want in the moment. However, as important as it is for women to not pre-judge themselves or a night's events, it is equally as important for you to be open to any possibility – which is where curiosity can be a great tool. Be open and curious about her, the possibilities, and your own desires, and you won't be lost in an agenda – you will be present and ready.

Imagine you are with a woman and you lean in for

a kiss. You have no idea where her boundaries currently are so you begin moving through the sexual experience. As you begin kissing her lips, her face, her neck and shoulders, your hands also caress down her arms and up her back. You squeeze and trace her hips and allow your hand to slowly caress the sides of her breasts. You are building heat in her body instead of rushing right to any goal, continuing to practice embodied empathy, enjoying both your own and her arousal in the process. Slowly, your hand moves under her shirt and caresses her belly, you continue to move between looking at her and kissing her passionately, and you use a combination of light, feathery touch and deeper, more holding touch (which we explain more in the Chapter 9: Sensuality).

She may be touching your upper body as well, your shoulders and back and stomach. Eventually, you remove her shirt. You trace the edges of her bra, still kissing her and keeping contact with other parts of her body, her hips, her back and stomach. Finally, you reach around and remove her bra. You are still going slowly, tracing the edges of her breasts, hinting the palm of your hand across her nipples, you may bring in your lips with light kisses and move towards more intense touch such as licking or kissing. When you try to move down towards the button of her pants, she stiffens a bit or pulls back. If you can see her face, you may notice her facial expression tighten or flinch a little bit. This means you have found the current edge of her boundaries. Many men at this point might take her pull-back as a rejection and may figure, "I guess I'll try to go further next time."

If you stop here after only one attempt, however, the woman may take this as a rejection of *her*. She may feel you don't want her enough to keep trying or she may lose confidence in your ability to stay with her through her fears. If you are still interested in going further at this point, you have another option. You can remind yourself that her current boundaries are *not a rejection of you*, they are based on how warmed up she is, how much of her mind is still engaged in the process, how many negative messages she got about sex and what kinds of fears she has about what you think about her.

Instead of backing off, follow four steps:

1. **Breathe**. Keep connected and relaxed in your own body.

2. **Do not move your hand away from the boundary**. In this case, the boundary is the lower part of her stomach near the button of her pants (or her thigh if she is wearing a skirt, etc.), but do not push her further at this moment. Go back to kissing, eye- contact, breast-play and all over body caresses and continue to visit her button or her thigh. If she continues to tighten over and over at this same spot, this is probably how far you will go, but

your continued attempts indicate to her that you are very interested.

3. **If her body softens or you get other cues of heightened arousal during one of these attempts, keep going**. Allow yourself to slowly unbutton a button. Continue using feather touch on her lower belly or inner thigh. Just because she has given you permission to touch her pussy, this does not mean that you should dive right in to it – it means that you now have the opportunity to continue to show her that you are nuanced and skilled lover by teasing and warming her up. You may have to go through this process multiple times with each new boundary.

4. **Only go as far as *you* want to go.** Some women are ready to escalate the sexual experience faster than you are or to have sex earlier than you are ready. Going along with this is one sure path to sexual dysfunction. While men have had very strong messages about trying to go as far as they can every time, many men don't actually want this. Tune into yourself and go at your own pace.

Just as you are speaking to her body and inviting it into its own internal "yes," continue listening to your body and paying attention to your internal "no." As we talked about in section one, during this entire interaction, you should continue to ask your own body how far it actually wants to go. You may find that you would rather wait and get to know someone better, to let the sexual tension build more between you and to give your body time to adjust to each new level of sexual intimacy.

Even when you have been with a woman for a long time and she seems like she is not interested in having sex at the moment, this feeling may shift if you stay present, read her cues, speak to her body and learn how to keep seducing her for a lifetime. A key ingredient in this ongoing seduction is keeping her engine warm so she stays interested!

Keep Her Interested

One of the biggest and most painful myths perpetuated in our society is that, if you really love someone, sex just continues to stay hot and spontaneous like it was at the beginning of the relationship. We believe this myth causes more pain and suffering around couples' sexual relationships than just about anything else. The truth of the matter is, after the honeymoon phase is over it is possible to have a hot, intense and passionate connection with your partner for the rest of your time together *if, and only if,* you take the time to consciously create that in your relationship.

Research on women's sexuality comes to one consistent conclusion: *what turns women on most is to feel desired by their partner.* To maintain the sexual heat in your relationship, your partner needs to feel your desire for her both inside and outside of the bedroom; she needs to know it is there even when it is not leading directly to sex. During one of our men's workshops, we were explaining the need to maintain this flow of desire throughout a relationship and a look of epiphany swept over the face of one of the participants, "If you want her to be hot in bed, you have to keep her engine warm!" he exclaimed.

Many men complain that in long-term relationships their partners become completely uninterested in sex. There is an important difference between men and women when it comes to sex and intimacy. To understand this difference, first imagine you have just had a fight with your girlfriend, you are still pretty pissed off at her because nothing has really been resolved. She goes into the bedroom, changes into her hottest negligee and high-heels and struts through the living room. Chances are, you are going to forget the fight and your resulting emotions and have sex with her.

This is generally not true for women. When women feel far away from their partners emotionally, when their relationships lack a consistent stream of connection and intimacy, and when they don't feel the ongoing force of your desire, they are much less likely to stay interested in sex. It is also important to keep in mind that the things that turn women on and keep them interested are probably different than the things that turn you on. A lot of men out there simply wait for bedtime after not having touched, complimented, kissed, listened to or connected with their partner in any way and expect her to be ready for sex.

In day-to-day living it is very easy to get preoccupied with all of the responsibilities that you have at work or at home. You may be making lists in your mind of what you need to do tomorrow, or be worrying about the car payment. When you are preoccupied, planning or problem solving, you may forget to notice the beautiful woman you are with. You might have checked her off the list, thinking "Good, I have a wonderful woman, I am happy, she is happy, everything is going fine, here is one thing at least that I don't have to worry about."

We are not telling you that you have to be thinking about her all the time, but we are telling you that it is never safe to check her off of the list of priorities. If you forget to show her how much she means to you for too long, she may silently build resentments without you even knowing it. She may become passive aggressive or frustrated, but may not feel it is okay for her to ask for what she needs. It is very difficult to ask for intimacy and perhaps even more difficult to give it to someone because they are asking for it which means that you need to be proactive. Stay curious to what her intimacy needs are as well as to your own needs. When you feel an opportunity for connection rely on your

Cockfidence and act on it.

Every day there are an infinite number of opportunities to let your partner know that you feel attracted, connected or, if you are at that phase in your relationship, in love with her. Letting your partner know that you desire her can be done by looking in her eyes, spontaneously kissing the back of her neck or asking a question about her day. From afar, you can send her an email or text message telling her how beautiful she was this morning getting ready to go to work and how you can't wait to see her tonight. One tiny text like "I can just picture how beautiful you look right now" can go a long way. You can also give her little gifts or surprises; it is more important that they are thoughtful and show that you know something about her and what makes her happy than that they are extravagant. It is great to give a gift "just because" and not only on her birthday or an anniversary.

If you are at the point in a relationship where you have a little bit of distance from the honeymoon phase, you may have forgotten how good it feels to flirt with your partner. One of our clients once came in complaining that he and his wife had been having sex about twice a month, which was very distressing for him since he desired sex at least three times a week. We asked him, "Do you flirt with your wife?" He said, "No." "Try flirting with her," we said, "you might like it."

The next week, he came back and said, "You're not

going to believe this! I did the few things that you sug-
gested, flirted with her, played, tickled her when she was
getting too serious and brought her a flower home one
night. She was all over me; I couldn't believe it was that
simple. But, the craziest part of it was that I really en-
joyed it too. It felt like when we first started dating. I
didn't know I could still feel like that about her."

In general, women think about sex far fewer times a
day than men. In order to keep your partner interested
and excited, keep sex and romance on her mind. Begin
warming up her engine way before you are going to have
sex. In small ways let her know that you are connected
with her and that you desire her. Another way to rev her
engine is to tell her what sex is going to be like. You can
help bring her to her body's desires by telling her a story
about what you want to do to her. You might send a text
like, "Get ready for an long, slow make-out session tonight" or "Have you seen the handcuffs? I was planning
on using them when I got home." Make sure whatever
you promise you are willing to deliver.

Oftentimes, when a woman knows something sexy
and fun is waiting for her, she begins to anticipate the
sensations and stays more connected to her sexuality
throughout the day. When you encourage her with re-
minders, she starts thinking about what's coming, and is
more likely to be a bit warmed up before you even get to
her. When you pick her up for a date or come home, she

may already be turned on because she feels close to you as a result of the connections you've initiated during the day or throughout the week.

When you are generous with your partner in this way, you will be surprised how generous she wants to be with you. When she thinks to herself, "My man looks at me with desire in his eyes, he kisses me spontaneously in grocery stores, and when I come home at night, even after a long, rough day, he tells me how beautiful I am," the next thought will probably be, "I wonder how I can give to him as much as he gives to me?"

EXERCISE
The Big Flirt

If you really want to exercise your curiosity about what it feels like to connect with women, your biggest tool is the flirt. Flirting is great fun because you don't have to take it seriously and it doesn't have to *mean* anything; it is just a way to play and create rapport, and you can do it with any woman. A couple of great tools for rapport include matching people's body posture, eye contact, tone of voice, and speed. Flirting is a playful zone full of subtleties, light teasing and innuendoes. It is fun, relaxed banter where you allow desire to be in the mix without overtly focusing on it.

Here are three examples of flirtatious conversations you

might have with your partner, using three personality types, one of which you may be more your style:

Playful:

You: (tickle, pinch or grab her and raise an eyebrow) "What'cha up to?"

Her: "I'm....[whatever she is doing.]"

You: "Oh yeah? Wanna wrestle?"

Tough:

You: (standing at a doorway) "If you want to get through, you'll have to kiss the gatekeeper."

Her: "Oh really?"

You: "Oh really."

Sensual:

You: "Hold still, sweetheart, you have something near your eye." Lean in and take a fake (or real) eyelash away very slowly, caress her hair or brush your lips lightly across her cheek.

This week, try flirting with anything that moves and have fun with it. A flirt can be one sentence or an entire conversation. Flirt with the grocery clerk, the car rental woman, the airline stewardess, the waitress, and the high-powered executive walking her dog on the street. Don't forget that flirting is much more than the words you say – flirting is how you are in your body when you say it – present, confident and aroused. Here are a few examples of flirting out in the world:

Grocery Clerk: "You find everything you needed?"

You: "I did now."

Toll collector: "Hi."

You: "I bet you say that to all the cute guys."

You: (to a woman behind you in a coffee store line) "Trade you a cut in line for your smile."

You can also find multiple other examples of flirtatious banter in just about any romantic comedy.

Spontaneity (Creativity + Flexibility)

We have broken down spontaneity into its component parts – creativity and flexibility. Creativity is the ability to imagine, plan, and introduce exciting new ideas and experiences into your relationship with your partner. While you may or may not remember the line in the movie *As Good As It Gets*, just about every woman's heart skipped a beat when Jack Nicholson told Helen Hunt, "You make me want to be a better man." Women want to inspire you to be the best man you can be. To be a better man means trying new experiences and bringing parts of yourself out that you may have never shown someone before. Humans are very habitual creatures who spend most of their time engaging in experiences within their comfort zone. This is why so many people complain that their relationships have become boring and their sex lives have become repetitive.

Challenging yourself to break out of the habitual and comfortable is what makes you a unique, interesting and exciting person, but it can also feel risky. People often fear bringing in their creativity because they worry about rejection, embarrassment or, worst of all, being left. Yet playing it safe usually ends with either you or your partner feeling unfulfilled and unsatisfied. When you bring in new ideas, when you offer women experiences that they have never had before and when you are willing to take the risk, women see you as brave and they feel inspired and excited by you. Creativity is most powerful when it is combined with the other key component of spontaneity, flexibility.

Flexibility is the ability to roll with the punches, to change direction if something is not working, to take the lead without expectations about particular results, and to shift gears if necessary without feeling rejection, disappointment, frustration, blame or shame.

The sentence that defines flexibility is "I'm not attached to what I'm offering." When you bring something creative into an experience you are having with a woman, she may go along with it enthusiastically or she may not be interested *right now*. When you experience a woman who is not interested in a new idea or activity you are bringing, you can follow one of two paths. The one that many men follow is to become identified with what they are offering and then feel rejected or hurt when it's not received. They then distance or shut down, which only serves to make their partner feel deserted. This distancing takes you out of your confidence and your partner feels like it is not okay for her to express her preferences. A better option is to be flexible.

Being flexible means that you do not take her disinterest as a rejection of you; as long as she is there with you, allow yourself to assume that she wants you. She just may not be interested in what you are proposing. When you remember that her momentary disinterest does not mean that she will never want what you have offered (in fact, she may even become interested five minutes later when she has gotten used to the idea), then you stay connected with her. If you lose presence in this moment, you may not even be there five minutes later when she is ready. If you stay, you gain the opportunity to bring in another idea that is fun and exciting for both of you.

To be truly spontaneous, you must bring creativity and flexibility into all of your sexual experiences with women. In order to do this, it helps to have some idea of why women have sex and what they want to feel. In this chapter, we introduce you to an in-depth look at women's sexual desires and fantasies and how you can creatively bring them what they really want. This chapter gives you many tools so you can be flexible as well.

Understand Women's "Hottest Sexual Movies"

Nearly everyone walks in the world with one or more sexual "movies" – fantasies of how they would most love to be seduced and taken. The characters may change but the basic themes often stay the same. While most people have the ability to enjoy multiple forms of seduction, a person's primary sexual movie generally brings them the most pleasure and intensity. Women get most of their inspiration for their ideal movie from romantic or passionate films, while men often get theirs from porn.

Each woman has her own ideal seduction movie – an assortment of thoughts about the kind of seduction that she wants to experience with her partner. Many women have daydreams about how they want their relationships with men to look, and what kinds of looks, words, acts, and gestures would fill their hearts and wet their pussies, but they often don't identify these thoughts as fantasies because they are not overtly sexual. This is especially true for women whose ideal seduction fantasy is Romantic.

"I never fantasize," Jane said assuredly to us.

"Really? Have you ever thought about what your ideal date night might be?"

"Well, sure, my boyfriend Jorge and I used to go on these fun dates where he would pick me up, open the door for me, and whisk me off somewhere to eat

and dance. Sometimes, I imagine that we are going on these types of dates, we are both all dressed up and he brings me a bunch of Stargazer Lilies because he knows those are my favorite flowers. When he sees me, he tells me how gorgeous I am, I see this look of love in his eyes."

"Do you think if you went on dates like this you would feel more sexual towards him?" we asked.

"Are you kidding me?" she laughed, "At the end of those dates, I could barely wait to get home and attack him!"

"Have you ever told him about these desires?" we asked.

"No, not in so many words, I guess there is part of me that just wants it to come from him, plus I never really thought of them as a fantasy and we have been together for so long, it seemed to me that we were past this stage. Even if we go out to dinner now, mostly we just talk about what we are doing with the remodel on the house, or work or something."

When we asked her what she felt like after those dates, she replied, "Not like attacking him, if that's what you mean. I feel more like making a to-do list."

If Jorge had asked her what her fantasies were, he would have gotten nowhere, yet, with just a little bit of clarification, she explained what kind of date would lead her to her desire.

While the motivation for seduction should come from inside of you – from your desire, your body and your confidence – you see the most response from a woman if you learn how to translate your seduction of her into the language of her movie. If you share with her how you are feeling based on her movie, you are that much more likely to turn her on. Whether she is in touch with it and can explain it or not, each woman has a fantasy about her ideal sexual experience.

This brings us to the three main seduction movies that women have. Most women's fantasies include a man who is romantic, passionate, dominant, or some combination of the three. Women may have only one of these, may have a favorite, may have a combination of all three, and may want to experience different ones at different times. Sometimes you can go through all of them in one seduction and sexual encounter. If you really want to get *your* movie, the best way is to generously give her hers.

Find Out What She Wants to Feel

We have said a couple of times in this book that women go to sex to *feel* something and this is actually true for both men and women. Just about everyone has a fantasy or set of fantasies about what their best sexual experience would look like, yet people rarely share these desires with their partner. Each woman is unique and each woman goes to sex for her own personal motives, and we want to give you some framework to help understand what your woman wants from sex and how you can bring it.

The first aspect that you need to understand is what emotion women want to feel from a sexual experience. For most people, male or female, there are one or two central emotions they look for in their sexual experiences and they may or may not be aware of these themselves. For women, these emotions might include feeling desired, taken, loved, connected, seen, punished, praised, ravished, worthy, vulnerable, precious, powerful, etc.

Be the Star Of Her Movie

Let's pretend that having sex is like going to the movies. You like Red movies, your partner likes Blue movies, and every time you want to see a movie together, you compromise and see a Purple movie. The problem is, neither of you *really loves* purple movies and you come home every time not quite satisfied. Many couple's sex lives looks like this. If you are really lucky, your lover has a similar movie to yours, but this is actually fairly rare. This is why we invite you to help your partner identify her movie and for you to identify yours. Most people are scared to share their true fantasies – probably because sharing your fantasies is one of the most private and vulnerable risks you can take.

If you are with someone in a relationship or situation in which you feel like she would be comfortable talking openly about her sexual desires, see if you can initiate a conversation about your fantasies in which you both can share your deepest desires. When you describe your movies, picture the character(s), the action, the set and what each of you would like to feel. Then, create a safe space where you both can share this deepest part of yourself.

When you share your movies there are two *essential rules*:

1. **No Judgments** – Everyone's desires are beautiful expressions of the deepest parts of who they are. Some of these desires will be realized in their lives and some will not. However, sharing them can create connection and intimacy between you and your partner even if you decide not to partake in your partner's desires or they decide not to partake in yours. Whether or not you want to take part in them is a completely different issue. People often judge each other's fantasies because they don't want to be a part of them. They feel threatened by the desires, so they wish they didn't exist. When sharing desires, it is essential to remember that desires do not necessarily have to happen – it is not anyone's job to do anything they do not want to do. This brings us to the importance of boundaries.

2. **Boundaries** – You and your partner both have a

right to your boundaries. While it is a beautiful gift to give your partner to really dive into the role of guest star in her movie, you also have a right to decide which parts you are ready to try now, and which parts you might want to add in later. The same goes for her if she is trying your movie. There may be some parts you or she will never partake in, but a "no" now doesn't shut the door to anything forever. Either of you might just change your mind…

Because many women have no idea of what their fantasies are or how to describe them to you, we have included the three types of seduction to which women most powerfully respond. You can often find out what turns her on the most by watching different movies with her from these categories and seeing what seems to get her most emotional or turned on. Many women have a combination of two or three of these seduction movies and like different experiences at different times.

The Romantic Movie

The romantic movie is the most common movie in our culture, and almost all women respond in some way to romantic words and gestures. Even women who have passionate and/or dominant fantasies often want some kind of romance in the mix. We asked a client if he ever was romantic with his wife. He said he felt like he wasn't good at it, and added, "I guess I just figured I'd leave that to George Clooney."

"But," we replied, "you're the only George Clooney she's got."

If you are in a monogamous relationship with a woman, you are the only romantic figure she gets to experience and learning how to show your romantic side might be what gets her really excited. Jane's descriptions of her early dates with Jorge and her ideal romantic date have many of the aspects of a romantic seduction. They include one of the three gifts that most commonly symbolize romance, the gift of flowers. The other two are chocolate and jewelry. Our society has capitalized greatly on these romantic gestures, creating the holiday St. Valentines day out of them and putting you under the gun to deliver or deal with some hurt feelings.

If you truly know how to romance your partner, these gestures are non-essential; in fact, they often are used as a shortcut and end up taking the place of actual, deeply-felt romance and connection. Don't get us wrong, we aren't saying that you should never give your partner a romantic gift, but these gifts aren't really what she is looking for, though they may seem to satisfy her momentarily. What she is really looking for is the feeling that you know and understand her deeply, that you pay enough attention to her to know what she wants, and that you can give her these things without her ever having to tell you. They symbolize her preciousness and importance to you.

The romantic movie includes the feeling of being taken care of and deeply loved by you. You can see the rest of these in Jane's story as well. Jorge knows that Stargazer lilies are her favorite flower, and he knows that she likes to dance. He also "whisks her off" with language that indicates he is taking charge and taking care of her. What's more, he tells her how gorgeous she is and he has that look of love in his eyes.

In addition to the example of Jane's romantic fantasy, here is a more comprehensive list of romantic words and gestures you can share with your partner.

Romantic Words

Romantic words have to do with beauty, preciousness, abstract sentimentality, fulfillment of dreams, and eternal connections. Examples include:

- **Describing her beauty**: "You are more beautiful than any work of art."
- **Talking about how precious she is to you**: "Being close to you means more to me than anything in the world." (If you were to say, "Touching you means more to me…" that would be more passionate than romantic because it has to do with physical desire instead of emotional sentimentality.)
- **Telling her how she fulfills your deepest desires**:

Truth vs. Romance

In order to help you imagine yourself offering your partner romance, we want to explain the difference between truth and romance. When we talk to men about the romantic seduction movie, we see some of them go into their logical minds. Once a woman client in our office said to her partner, "I want to feel like you would die for me." Her husband looked at her like she was completely nuts. "Are you crazy, of course I wouldn't die for you! I am independent and I don't want to be with a child; I want someone who is independent too." Clearly, this man had not learned the difference between truth and romance. Romance is not "true" per se, it is a co-created fantasy between two people, that, when offered consciously and conscientiously, can be very fun and satisfying to each person. After all, his wife had her own job, friends and life and was not dependent on her husband; however, she was turned on by the idea that someone could want her so much they would die for her. She knew her husband wasn't about to throw himself in front of a bus for her, she just wanted the *feeling* of being wanted that badly. When you choose to express some of these sentiments, make sure you are only expressing those that align with your actual commitment to the person. For example, don't say, "I want to be with you forever" to a fuck-buddy, but, at the same time, allow yourself to offer words that are part of the fantasy, that express the intensity of your emotion and desire

> in a way that meets her fantasy desires, such as "I wish I could fuck you like this forever!"

"When I look at you, I see the woman of my dreams."

◆ **Talking about how your connection is beyond the bounds of time or space**: "I feel like I've known you forever, like we've always been together."

Romantic Gestures

◆ Put post-it notes around the house that say any romantic sentiments (fewer words are better) or with a picture or heart.

◆ Send a romantic email or text during the day.

◆ Give little sweet gifts like flowers, chocolate, earrings, etc.

◆ Remember special days: birthdays, anniversaries, the first day you kissed, the first time you met, etc.

◆ Surprise her with activities that take account of what she really loves – tell her to get dressed appropriately and then take her somewhere (i.e., dinner at her favorite restaurant, a hike to a beautiful lake, a drive to a romantic view, a night at the theater, dancing, a spa treatment, etc.)

◆ Stare deeply into her eyes without any agenda, show vulnerability and emotion.

- Find or write a poem or quote that reminds you of her or is about her.
- Give her soft, teasing kisses while touching her face or neck.

The Passionate Movie

When it comes to passion, the best way to describe it is *animalistic*. When we speak of animalistic sex, what we mean is sex that is a bit out of control. In this society, we spend years socializing our children out of animal-like behavior. Passion begins when the part of your brain that tells you to be self-conscious and courteous and a good boy shuts down, and then out comes the part that holds itself back, that wants to bite, grab and growl, and to satisfy all of your senses, as you dive into one another.

Nothing captures the idea of the passionate seduction more than the passionate kiss, depicted in so many movies by this time it might look cliché to you, but it doesn't look or feel cliché to women. It is important to begin with a passionate look, letting all of the animalistic desire come in to yours eyes and hold it before jumping right into a kiss. If you go too quickly to the kiss, you don't allow any tension and excitement to build. When you wait, you allow yourself and her to build into a frenzy of desire where you can't rip each other's clothes off fast enough. Make sure you aren't spilling your passion all over her; at the beginning, hold it in your eyes, and

Rape Fantasies

About 80% of women fantasize about rape. Let us be clear here, women **DO NOT** actually want to be raped, however, in a rape fantasy the woman does not have to take responsibility for the sexual experience. In a rape fantasy, she has not made a conscious decision to have sex and therefore does not have to worry that she might be seen as a slut. In addition, rape fantasies allow women to **SAFELY** explore their desire for aggressive sex. She can play with the idea of experiencing men's animalistic desires as opposed to experiencing the actual terror and pain that comes from real rape. Some women even like to play these fantasies out with their partners in a safe and boundaried environment.

You might ask yourself, why would a woman fantasize about something she doesn't actually want to do? There are many reasons for this. In fantasies about rape the woman might actually imagine herself in the role of the man, therefore experiencing a sense of power she may have lost when she was violated. Thus, a woman might have a fantasy that turns them on that is violating or painful, they don't want anyone to get hurt, but they want to feel the full force of their arousal.

invite her energy to come to you. When you feel she is locked in, then set your inner animal free.

There are some common pitfalls with passion. You

may fear that desiring women in this way is objectifying and that she will feel like you only want her for sex. On the contrary, being desired intensely is one of women's most common fantasies. At the same time, she also wants to know that you are connected to her. You do this by bringing in eye contact, saying her name passionately, or commenting specifically on the things that drive you crazy about her.

You may also fear that bringing this kind of energy will overwhelm a woman as though women are delicate and easily broken. This could cause you to hold back your passion, especially if you feel that you have too much or that it will not be received. On the contrary, most women's bodies are strong enough to receive all the passion you have in your body for her and more. She may be surprised by it at first, which is why it takes confidence to stay with the feeling and not allow her embarrassment or surprise to pull you both out of it. Instead, with your passionate look and your focused confidence, you pull her into the hottest experiences you have ever had.

Passionate Words

Passion has to do with immediacy, intensity of desire, animalistic need, uncontrollable urges, and overwhelming feelings. Examples include:

- **Talking about how she brings out the animal in you**: "I could eat you alive right now."

- **Sharing the intensity of your physical need**: "I can't wait to be inside you."
- **Telling her how strongly you feel about her**: "When you are near me, my heart feels like it is going to explode."
- **Talking about how her pleasure and her body delights you**: "When I feel you come, energy shoots through my whole body; I could spend hours just licking and tasting you."

Passionate Gestures

- Throwing her up against a wall on a walk or at home and kissing and touching her passionately. (It can be great to do this in public sometimes as long as she is open to it; it means you can't wait until you have her alone, you have to have her *right now*.)
- Looking at her with an intensity of desire in your eyes like you can't hold back any longer.
- Shouting out your window, "I'm with the sexiest woman in the world and I want everyone to know it!"
- Having a lovemaking session where you make sure that you kiss, lick, bite, smell or suck every inch of her body. Make sure you suck on her toes and fingers and don't miss a single spot.

The Dominant Movie

Many women have fantasies of being taken by a powerful man who knows exactly what he wants and isn't afraid to take her there. We talk quite a bit about dominance in this book not because all women have dominant fantasies, but because dominance can be a touchy subject that needs lots of finesse. Some women who have dominance as one of their movies or their primary movie can be very ambivalent about these desires, and it is important whenever you are playing in the area of dominance and submission or role-play where there are power differences that you be aware that this kind of play can provoke strong emotions. Not all women are ready for dominance, and some need to feel a romantic or passionate connection before they are willing to even explore it. Some women like light dominance but nothing too heavy, and some women *never* want to play this way.

Many woman who believe in women's equality feel that they should not want to be submissive in the bedroom or that this power dynamic might end up leaking into other parts of their relationship. The truth is, there are power differences in relationships and dominance and submission can be one way to openly explore these differences. This is why we also recommend switching roles and seeing what it feels like for each of you to be on the other side of this equation, where she is the dominant and you are the submissive.

There are a number of pitfalls that men experience when bringing dominance into a sexual situation. You may be worried that it is degrading to your partner and that no woman really wants this. There is a difference between really being mean and abusive and *playing* with dominance. When a woman wants this kind of play, she does not feel abused at all, quite the contrary, she feels *taken care of* and *accepted.*

It might sound strange to think that spanking a woman or calling her a "dirty slut" or a "good little girl" is taking care of her. Try this: imagine your deepest most exciting fantasy and then imagine a woman offering that fantasy to you. Think of how cared for and accepted you would feel.

Sometimes men also fear that being dominant and bringing out this side of themselves will cause them to lose control. Many men have a deep mistrust for the more intense side of their personality – as we talked a lot about in relationship to anger in the first section. If you have a lot of unprocessed anger, it may be very important for you to work with your anger with a therapist in order to begin to process and feel trust for all of the different aspects of your personality. Knowing you can stay in control is an important first step if you are going to engage in this kind of play. You can also begin with very light play and see what happens in that arena before going further.

Power play of any kind takes trust, and if you are moving out of light dominance like an occasional spank or hair-pull into more advanced power play then you also need to communicate about desires and boundaries and have a safeword. A safeword is any word that you would not normally use during a sexual experience that indicates that one partner is uncomfortable with what's going on and that the play needs to stop. Many people use words like "yellow" (to indicate slow down) and "red" (to indicate stop), while others have their own personal word, which may also have personal resonance or humor for them, such as "zucchini" or "mouse." The reason you use a word other than "stop" or "no" is that you may want to be able to use those words as part of the play to make it feel more realistic.

In addition to establishing a safe word, to really get to what kind of dominant fantasy she has, you may need to ask her a lot of questions about what words she wants to hear and what kinds of actions she wants you to take. It is also helpful for you to talk about and practice with her pain threshold if you are going to be doing rougher play like spanking, hair-pulling or flogging. If she is uncertain, then make an agreement to test some words and actions out and then afterwards talk about what worked and what didn't.

It is important that both you and your partner know that it is very rare to get the dominant movie right the first time. You need to be prepared to have a number of "takes" in order to find out what words and actions turn her on the most. If she tells you something turns her on, for example, she says, "I really like it when you tell me to get on my knees and suck your cock," it is important to ask her what turns her on about it. Then you begin to get some insight into why particular actions turn her on and add in other actions that are similar thematically. It is also not just the words, but the tone and attitude that are important.

She may say, for example, "I like it because I feel as though you are in control of the experience and I have to do exactly what you say." On the other hand, she might say, "I like it because it feels like you are using me for your pleasure." These are two very different fantasies that would lead to different kinds of sexual experiences. The first could include pleasing both you and her but you staying completely in charge. The second would mean that you want to focus more on taking for your own pleasure; if you focus too much on hers she might get turned off.

No matter what parts you are playing it is important to remember that dominance is not about going crazy or being mean. The attitude of dominance is actually a very slow, centered, calm and powerful place from which to approach a woman. When you are dominant, you are in complete control so you can take your time, go slow, be stern sometimes and gentle others, punish sometimes and reward other times. Dominance is different from anger; when you are dominant, there is nothing to be angry about, you are in control and your submissive will do what you say. If she gets out of line, you can always punish her. So, breathe deeply, relax and figure out exactly what you want.

Dominant Words

Dominant words communicate a feeling of command, control, confidence, power over, and being in the position of giving and taking away permission or offering praise or punishment, or degrading. Deliver words with a calm, commanding tone and do not ask, but tell her what to do. It is very different to say, "Please turn around and get on your knees" than it is to say, "Get on your knees and stick your ass in the air." When in a dominant role, use commands and avoid prefacing these commands with "I want you to" or "Will you?" Of course she will, she is at your mercy. If she won't, she always has her safeword to stop you.

- ◆ **Command statement:** "Spread your legs and show me your pussy."
- ◆ **Taking away permission:** "Did I tell you it was okay to look at me? Look at the ground."
- ◆ **Offering praise:** "You've been a very good girl, come here and I'll stroke your hair."

- **Degrading:** "You are a dirty little slut."
- **Disapproving:** "You call that masturbating? Stick your fingers inside yourself."

Dominant Gestures

- **Spanking** – especially as a punishment or to take her to her edge of intense sensation.
- **Choking** – or, more accurately, holding the throat. The center of the throat should not receive any pressure and you can put light pressure on the sides of the neck. Do not cut off her air or press the veins on the sides of her neck too hard.
- **Hair-pulling** – or, more accurately, hair-holding. Best done by combing your fingers into the hair at the nape of the neck close to the scalp and making a fist. For greatest sensual impact, hair holding should always be entered into slowly and released slowly.
- **Tying her up** – with handcuffs, scarves or ropes. You can tie either arms or legs or both, just make sure you tie her in a way that you can reach all your favorite parts and check to make sure blood is circulating to hands and feet throughout the play.
- **Blindfolding** – takes away her ability to know what's coming next and puts you in full control of her body.

Combine the Movies and Bring Sensuality

Just because you are engaging in a passionate or dominant seduction does not mean that you should throw your sensuality out the window. It is the combination of taking charge and having excellent technique that satisfies the depths of a woman's sexual longing. Animalistic squeezing and grabbing can be combined with light touches and kisses to make it even more intense and tantalizing. Dominance is an attitude and it is not abusive; you can be dominant with a smile on your face, a gentle touch or even a whisper. In any sexual experience, you can move from intense passion to slow seduction and then build up into dominance allowing both of your bodies the time it takes to really let arousal grow. The longer you play and build, the more intense your connection and orgasms will be. Be creative, be spontaneous and be patient – getting it right takes time.

Make Her the Star of Your Movie

In the same way that you may get very aroused by a woman's turn on, women also get turned on by seeing you at the height of your sexual arousal. Since it is extremely rare that partners in a relationship have exactly the same movie, in order to give your partner the delight of seeing you at the height of your pleasure, you need to make her the star of your movie as well.

Making her the star of your movie means communicating what you want and initiating the kind of sex that gives you the greatest turn on. It also means allowing yourself to dive fully into your own sensation, pleasure and experience of sex. Some men are so focused on turning their partners on that they lose track of themselves. If you find that you are in your mind a lot worrying about what your partner wants and whether she is okay, you may become disconnected from your body and its sensations. In the long run, this can lead to erection and ejaculation problems.

Finding balance between focusing on your partner and yourself during sex, by searching inside of yourself to find out what you really want and then incorporating your hottest movie into your sex life with a partner keeps your libido and your sexual function at their highest level. When you really own your own desires in a sexual relationship and share them with your partner, you allow all of yourself into the experience and long-term satisfaction is at your fingertips.

Spontaneity is the combination of creativity and flexibility – by moving between these two qualities, life continues to be full of fun. A *Cockfident* man has fun and makes mistakes – he is not focused on doing things perfectly. The movie analogy is an apt one because, in creating your movies together, you get lots of takes to get the scene right, and eventually the movie flows.

Spiritual Seduction Movie

Recently, in the U.S., there has been a contingent of sexuality educators who teach what they call "Tantra," but could more correctly be referred to as "Neo-Tantra" or "Sacred Sexuality." The idea behind these teachings is a wonderful one, that our sexuality is actually a sacred part of who we are and that the expression of that sexuality is an expression of our connection with our spiritual self.

We use some of the tools from these teachings such as breathwork and the idea that sexuality is an energetic exchange. However, we avoid calling one set of sexual practices sacred because some might take this to mean that this way of being sexual with someone is somehow more sacred than other sexual practices. We believe that two people sharing romance, passion, dominance/submission or some combination of all of these can also be profound and sacred. The sacredness of a sexual act has more to do with the intention and connection of the actors than with the practices themselves.

This being said, there are a small but growing number of women whose primary seduction fantasy is a spiritual seduction. These women want to feel like goddesses and be worshipped as such and they want to feel like you are a representation of the divine as well. Spiritual sexuality focuses on breathing together, honoring one another through rituals such as dance, incense and candle-lighting, intention-setting, and conscious connection. Sexual acts in this movie often focus on the giving and receiving of sexual massage, and intend to heal or build energy in the body.

EXERCISE
"Sleeping Beauty": Three Seduction Movies in One

For this exercise, we offer three different movies that begin the same way so that you can compare them and see which ones are most arousing to you. You can also show them to a partner or a female friend and discuss what excites her most. Use these movies as a guide to begin spontaneously creating your own scenes. These movies are all told from the woman's point of view. They are short, but action packed; when you practice them with a partner, take your time with each caress, kiss, squeeze, etc. You will want to make sure her body is fully responsive (remember the non-verbal cues!), before you begin touching her pussy.

ROMANTIC SEDUCTION MOVIE

I'm lying in bed half-asleep, feeling warm and cozy. My partner slowly enters the room, moving quietly so as not to disturb my restfulness. He comes and gently lies beside me and begins to stroke my hair and comb his fingers through it. He leans in and whispers in my ear, "You look so delicate sleeping there, I can barely believe that I get to have someone so beautiful in my bed." He begins to give me soft kisses on my cheeks and lips, touching my face lightly with his hand. He takes his time with every inch of me, as though each part deserves as much adoration as the next.

I begin to feel my body getting warmer as the kisses slowly become deeper. I can feel how precious he thinks I am as he kisses down my neck. He runs a finger across my collarbone saying, "When I see you across a room, I'm always drawn to your long neck and collarbone, they are so majestic." He kisses gently down my belly, tracing the side of my body with one hand like he is exploring me for the first time all over again.

As he moves down to kiss my thighs, his hand reaches to my feet, cupping and massaging them gently. He seems to know each part of me intimately, knowing what kinds of touch feel good on every part. My hips begin to rock slowly as I anticipate where his gentle kisses up my thigh will lead. He kisses me slowly across my pussy then up across my belly again, back to my lips, then back down.

His lips and tongue softly explore my pussy lips. A few times he looks up at me, catching me looking down at him and soaking in our connection, then he stays with my pussy, and I can feel him savoring each moment. He seems to feel the same way about my pussy as the rest of me, completely delighted. I have my first orgasm while he is licking me. "I want you on top of me" I pant.

He teases me a few more times with his tongue across my pussy lips and then moves on top of me sliding slowly but deeply inside of me. As he thrusts gently yet forcefully in and out, he looks in my eyes, then kisses me, then whispers in my ear, "You are everything I've always dreamed of." The words fill my ear just as I'm moving to my second orgasm and he thrusts faster, increasing the flood of wetness in my pussy. He moves back down to lick my pussy again and I get ready for a nice, long, slow ride...

PASSIONATE SEDUCTION MOVIE

I'm lying in bed half-asleep when I hear him open the front door downstairs and come inside. I had decided to surprise him in my new red garter and panties, but had fallen asleep while waiting. My heart begins to beat faster as I hear him coming up the stairs, moving quickly like he can't wait another moment. When he opens the door, I am lying there, in my sexy outfit on top of the covers, posed and waiting. He gasps when he sees me, looking at me like a lion about to devour an elk.

Suddenly he is on top of me and I feel like he has eight hands. I am completely lost in his embrace, as his hands grab my hips and thighs. He is kissing my lips, my neck, and my chest, moaning my name breathily between each kiss. He starts licking my armpits and smelling them, "God, I love your smells, the way you taste, I can't get enough of you."

I begin to grab him back, his arms and his ass, like I'm holding on for dear life as he consumes every inch of me. He flips me over and begins kissing and biting the back of my neck and shoulders. I can feel his heavy breath between each bite as he tickles and squeezes my ass and thighs. He turns me over again, diving this time into my pussy, he buries his face between my legs and I feel his tongue, his lips, his nose. He wants me all over his face and, at the same time, his hands are still exploring my breasts and hips. First one finger and then two fingers tease inside of me as he continues to tongue my clitoris and lips.

His fingers are moving all the way to my cervix and his tongue moves faster and faster across my pussy. As I come, he presses even further inside me with his fingers as I moan, tears are coming out of the corners of my eyes and I am laughing, feeling all of the emotions flood at once. He comes up and begins kissing me and I can taste myself on his lips. He rolls me on top of him and I guide his cock inside of me with my hand, moving just the way I need to so I can press my clit onto his pelvis. He is grabbing my hips to support my thrusting, then cupping my breasts. I move back towards his mouth, feeling our tongues swirl together again as I have another orgasm. "I can't wait any longer, you turn me on so much," he says, and comes deep inside my pussy.

DOMINANT SEDUCTION MOVIE

(Don't forget, this movie requires an established safe word!)

I'm lying in bed half-asleep when I hear him come into the bedroom. He shuts the door firmly behind him and locks it. He lies down behind me and with a very calm, slightly stern voice, says, "Don't move or speak, just nod if you understand. For the next hour, you are going to do exactly what I say. If you step out of line or make a mistake, you will be punished. Do you understand?" I nod quickly, already beginning to feel the heat between my legs and he hasn't even touched me yet. He rolls me on to my stomach, and pulls my hips up so my ass is in the air.

"I like you in this position, I can see your pussy and you are at my mercy. Arch your back so your ass is tilted in the air." I feel this sense of surrender inside of me, I want to please him and do exactly what he says. He doesn't think it's high enough, "Stick it up higher," he says with a firm slap on my right ass-cheek. I arch higher. "Perfect," he praises me. He begins to play back and forth between lightly caressing my hips and ass then pinching my nipples firmly. If I begin to relax too much, he slaps me on the ass reminding me to keep it high, "Spread your legs a little wider now so I can see you better."

He takes two fingers and puts them up to my mouth, "Get them nice and wet so I can play with your pussy." I begin to suck his fingers making sure to get them fully wet. I'm up on my hands and knees now with my back arched towards his hand as he lightly strokes my pussy, then squeezes my pussy lips, then lightly strokes again. He takes my hair in his fist and moves my head towards his cock. "If you are a good girl and suck it just right, you will get a special treat." I do my best to please him as he directs me, moving my head just the way he likes it, "Yes, that's good."

I suck it for a few more minutes and then he hands me a vibrator, "Once I'm all the way inside you, you can put it on your clit," he says. I get greedy and put in on my clit right away. He begins spanking me and pinching my nipples but I come before I surrender to his punishment. "You are a naughty little slut and now you are going to get fucked." I am soaking wet by now as he shoves his cock inside of me. I'm working the vibrator and I can feel a lubed up finger playing with my asshole as he is fucking me. Just as his finger begins to move inside my ass I come again, begging him not to stop.

QUALITY 9

Sensuality

ensuality is an approach to sexual connection that utilizes all the senses: sight, touch, taste, smell, and hearing. Sensuality is indicated by a willingness to go slow, give varied touch, and enjoy the stimulation of all of your and your partner's senses in a sexual experience. It is predicated on the ability to focus on each delectable moment of a sexual interaction and to let go of orgasm as the only or ultimate goal of sex. When women describe their best sexual experiences, they almost always express detailed descriptions of sensual acts such as kissing, touching or being looked at with desire. When you bring sensuality to a woman, you are catering to her body's longings.

Market with Your Kissing Skills

"Was he a good kisser?" It is one of the most common

questions we ask our girlfriends after the first date. If the answer is "no" we nod sadly, knowing that the likelihood of a second date is pretty much nil. To be clear, there aren't really "good kissers" and "bad kissers" per se; more than anything else there are compatible kissers and incompatible kissers (however, if you are very nervous during a kiss, you might keep your lips really tight or closed, which is not a great approach to kissing). When you come across as an innovative and inspired kisser, you are giving her a taste of where she can expect to go with you sexually. There are some fantastic kissing techniques that can show your prowess and there are also ways to match your kissing style to a partner's, allowing you to become a compatible kisser even if you don't start out that way.

The first rule of kissing is that kisses have a beginning, middle, and end. Some people start out a kiss in the middle, leaning in with their mouths wide open, tongue already sticking out. It is possible that you may meet another kisser just like this and then it all works out, but, if your partner is not ready this may feel too wet and intrusive all at once. In order to move into compatible kissing, start with slow, soft-lipped, closed-mouth kissing and then move into opening your mouth and allowing your tongue to gently explore her mouth and tongue. Sense into her pace and movement and see how it feels in relation to your own. To come to the end of this kiss, allow your lips to come back together and gently end with closed mouth kisses. You don't have to stop here but can continue moving through this opening and closing over and over again. Try varying the speed of your kiss as well as the depth of your kiss, moving your tongue more deeply in her mouth and reading her non-verbal cues to see how she responds. Other very arousing variations include licking her lips, kissing the corners of her mouth, and nibbling and sucking on her lips. Also try moving from lips to cheeks, ears and neck and then returning back to the lips again.

There is a great turn-taking game you can try to improve your kissing compatibility. Tell your partner to lie down on the bed and pretend she can't move at all, and to keep her mouth soft, not rigid. Use all of the kissing techniques we have talked about above but without her kissing back. Kiss and tease her lips softly with your mouth. Lick and nibble her lips, kiss her face and neck, always returning to her lips. Part her lips with your tongue and explore her tongue and teeth. Suck on her lips and taste her mouth. Then have her give feedback about what she liked best. Now it's her turn. As she kisses you, pay attention to her technique and style, usually people kiss the way they want to be kissed.

Build a Foundation of Sensation

Making love to a woman is like playing a symphony; you have to create a foundation of sound before you can move to the powerful crescendos. When you give a woman enough time for a foundation of sensation to build, you set the stage for extraordinary passion and explosive multi-orgasms. At the beginning of any sexual encounter most women need their whole bodies warmed up before rushing right to the breasts, clitoris, or G-Spot. One of our favorite rules to live by in sex is: "If you are touching her clitoris before it is ready, you might as well be rubbing her nose – that's as much sensation as she is going to get from it." Touching her clitoris or G-Spot too soon can actually have a numbing effect, making it take longer for her to orgasm than it would have if you had taken the time to warm up her whole body. Instead of rushing in, you can build your partner a foundation of sensation in her body. Even though all women are different, when you approach any woman's body to warm it up, there are some excellent guidelines based on female and human physiology to which the great majority of women respond.

Move from Periphery to Center

When you start a sexual encounter with a woman, begin with the periphery and move to the center. Think of "the center" as her pussy and breasts (and asshole if that is part of your sex play) and the rest of her body is "the periphery." When you move from periphery to center, each stroke and touch and squeeze on other parts of her body sends teasing messages to her pussy, creating anticipation and saying, "I'll be there soon, you'll just have to wait for me..." When you move from periphery to center, you give her pussy time to fill with arousal, warm up, and lubricate.

Caress Her Entire Body

To warm her up, caress her entire body, and as always – stay in touch with her non-verbal cues. This way, you can map her pleasure zones from periphery to center and keep abreast of your partner's specific pleasures and desires. Explore long, all-over body touch that includes her hair, arms, back, legs, butt and stomach. Remember, her desires can change throughout a day, the month and during any single sexual experience so you need to be open to changes in what turns her on and to keep coming to each experience with all of your Extraordinary Lover Qualities.

Hair

Touching her hair can be both soothing and very arousing. When you touch her hair, either stroke over the hair or run your fingers through it like a comb; each woman likes her hair touched and stroked differently.

Neck and Ears

Start with kissing and light bites on her neck and

ears. Focus especially on the back of the neck and shoulders for biting. Some people really like blowing and licking around their ears, for others it is irritating – notice body language and cues.

Back

The back loves long, slow feathery touches, especially around the upper back and neck, along the sides of her body and hips. When you run your fingers across her back make sure to give feather touch to the back of her neck.

Thighs

The thighs, and especially the inner thighs, offer a great opportunity for teasing because you can get close to her pussy but not touch it. This increases anticipation and helps her love her thighs even more. Run your fingers or tongue up her inner thighs without moving across her pussy.

Bellies

Many women do not feel comfortable about their bellies; they were told that their bellies aren't attractive. No matter how it looks to you, your partner may feel that her belly is too big or soft. Women are used to sucking in their stomachs, which stops them from breathing in deeply. Shallow breathing cuts of the circulation of sensation and pleasure in the body by lowering oxygen levels and separating her from the lower regions of the body. Helping a woman love her belly helps her relax and breathe down more deeply. Positive verbal messages about her belly combined with touches, kisses, nibbles and licks all help her to love and integrate this part of her body. She might resist at first, but when you show your enthusiasm towards her belly, she may eventually be able to let go. Touch her belly lightly, kiss and caress it, lick circles around her bellybutton. Move to the horizontal line where her belly ends and her mons begins – this is a very sensitive area that can enjoy feather touch and light licking.

Pay Special Attention to Her Hot Spots

Most women have hot spots that are more sensitive, including the backs of her knees and inner elbows, her armpits, the back of her neck, under and around the sides of her breasts, the lower part of her stomach near her panty line, the sides of her body, her inner thighs, her ass cheeks and her toes. Take time to visit each of these hot spots, exploring them slowly with your hands, your lips, your tongue and your teeth.

Armpits

Armpits can be particularly powerful areas of exploration because they have so many sensitive nerve endings and rarely receive touch. If she is not wearing deodorant and is not too ticklish, try touching, licking, biting and smelling her armpits. If she has never had this experience she might get a little bit embarrassed. This is because the armpits are another part of her body associated with shame. If she has this response, stay with it and give her a chance to relax into it. She may be able to let go of some of that shame and find a lot of pleasure and sensations she didn't know she could feel.

Breasts

Part of moving from periphery to center is starting with the periphery of the breasts, which are, for many women, the most sensitive part of the breast. Stroke around the sides and under her breasts well before moving to her nipples. This gives her body the powerful message that you are willing to take your time and that you care about her pleasure. Remember, women have different sensitivity in their breasts at different times of the month and in different times in a sexual encounter. At the beginning she might enjoy feather touch, licking, blowing air and brushing your finger on her nipple, later she might prefer that you pinch her nipples harder, twist them or pull them. As we mentioned above, don't limit your attention to the nipple – there is a lot more to explore. Cupping her breasts or circling from the outside can be very pleasurable. Her breasts are a great place to use ice and warm water. Try putting an ice-cube in your mouth and then sucking her nipple, then do the same with warm water (this can also be great for oral sex!).

Vary Your Touch

Make sure you vary your touch and don't linger too long on each spot. Any single part of the body, if touched for an extended period of time in the exact same way, numbs out. You can feel this if you take your finger and rub it across any two-inch patch of skin on your hand or arm for thirty seconds. At first, you might feel the sensation, however, if you keep doing the same motion over and over again, sensation is soon lost.

The hottest sex happens when sexual tension builds higher and higher through varied touch and sensual surprises. To vary sensation we offer a number of touches below. You can try blowing on her body with pursed lips for cool air or blowing close to her body with your mouth more open for warm air. Also use props such as feathers, silken scarves, ice or warm water.

Begin with Feather Touch

At the beginning of any sexual encounter, when the body first starts to warm up, it is generally good to start with light touch. If she is ticklish you will need to begin with combination touch (see below) or a heavier touch. The lightest and most arousing touch is called feather touch and it can be used on any part of the body to begin to get it to tingle. Feather touch is done with the

The Ticklish Tendency

The only time you should avoid using extremely light or "feather touch" is when your partner is very ticklish. Ticklishness is often a sign of someone who has pleasure anxiety and it is possible to become less ticklish through practice. Your partner may or may not be willing to confront her ticklishness. If she wants to work with the edge of ticklishness, you can practice combining deep, holding touch with feather touch in small increments while encouraging her to breathe deeply and connect with the sensation in her body. You can also use one hand for a deeper "grounding" touch while exploring feather touch nearby with the other hand. If she is not interested in this kind of change, begin with deeper touch at the beginning. As she becomes more aroused, she may be able to handle lighter touch.

fingertips and fingers; the palm can be used as well as long as you can keep it held barely touching the skin. In addition to fingertips, you can also achieve light touch by using the backs of your fingers and hands. The backs of the hands are great to use if you ever get sweaty palms.

While many people think of massage as a great prelude to sex, remember that massage is relaxing as opposed to arousing touch. If your partner is very stressed out, it may be helpful to invite her into her body with massage, but if you want it the experience to go to sex as opposed to sleep, once she is relaxed and present, you should move to lighter and more arousing feather touch.

Because men's hands are generally larger and heavier than women's hands, and they may not have had a lot of practice with activities like combing another person's hair or stroking a baby's skin, it is hard to imagine how lightly women like to be touched. If you are a bit heavy-handed, try barely touching her body at all. Remember, feather touch is arousing – "massaging" touch is not. Whether you are giving your partner the lightest, most sensual touch or squeezing her ass with your full strength, all of your touch should be connected with her and with your own body – it should be *Cockfident*.

Move to Holding, Intense Touch, and Combination Touch

As a woman's body gets more aroused, so does her threshold for sensation. At the beginning of a sexual encounter, start with light touch and slow caresses then bring in more firm or intense touch as her arousal level gets higher. When you are starting out, you want to start with light touch that wakes up the body. Later, to intensify sensation you can shift between the light touch and holding, intense touch, and combination touch.

Holding

Holding is applying a touch and keeping it there for a few breaths (at least 3) without any movement. While feather touch arouses the body, holding grounds the body encouraging arousal to spread through and sink deeper into the body. Holding also allows a woman to let go and relax. It helps her trust your touch and that you will give her time to unfold her sexuality. There are a number of ways you can hold the body to ground it.

Hair "Holding"

Hair holding or hair pulling can be a very irritating and painful experience if done incorrectly. We call it hair "holding" to contrast it to some of the kinds of hair-pulling that are often shown in porn, where a woman is grabbed by the ends of her hair or a pony-tail and her neck is pulled back into an uncomfortable or danger-ous position as her hair is yanked. Hair holding is quite different and can be very grounding and sensual. Bring your hand to the back of her neck, spread your fingers and comb your fingers up through the back of her hair close to her scalp. Then, simply make a fist, keeping your hand close to the scalp. Make sure you make the fist slowly, hold for a minute or so, and then slowly release the fist. Never move into or leave hair-holding quickly or you lose all of the grounding and spreading sensations that it has to offer. Hair holding is a great one for com-bination touch (below).

Waist Holding

Another part of a woman's body that responds excellently to holding is the waist, right above the hips. To hold a woman's waist, start by caressing her down the sides of her body until you get to her waist and then contrasting the sensation with a grab. Cup your hands a bit and grab her waist, holding tightly for a few breaths before letting go. The wonderful bonus about waist-holding is that it gives you the ability to show your skills and confidence, because it puts you in a position where you can lift your partner's body so her back is arched and/or move it into different positions.

Ass Holding (and Inner Thigh Holding)

When it comes to approaching an ass cheek, you have to grab it like you mean it. Take a nice big handful and give it a good squeeze and then hold on. Do not massage it or open and close your fist, and keep the following thought in mind, "Your ass is mine." This helps you avoid grabbing her ass too tentatively or non-sexually and losing your opportunity for her full response. Asses can take a nice, strong grab, probably stronger than you think! Ask for feedback. This same kind of holding can be done on the inner thigh though inner thighs can be more sensitive so don't squeeze them too hard.

Intense touch

When the body is more aroused and excited, bring in more intense touch. Every woman has a different sensation threshold and, as pleasure hormones get released into the body, women's sensations thresholds change. As you move to higher levels of arousal, and there are more endorphins released into the body, more intense touch added into the mix may serve to intensify pleasure. When you are adding more intense touch, make sure you are interweaving it with other types of touch. Giving too much intense touch consistently can cause the body to numb out and become desensitized. To put this in the context of women's hottest movies, The Romantic Movie likely would include the least amount of intense touch, while the Passionate Movie can include greater amounts of intense touch. You can incorporate the most intense touch into the Dominant Movie.

Biting

Biting can be an extremely sexy and stimulating experience for both the biter and the bitten – an idea that vampire movies have exploited many times over. Biting is an art that can bring extraordinary pleasure to the body, and it has been known to be responsible for many fantastic goose bumps. Biting should be paired with light kissing and licking for the greatest effect. The best places for biting are the back of the neck right where it slopes down to the shoulder, other parts of the neck and shoulders and ass cheek. Don't be afraid to bite hard – just make sure your hard bites are short bites and then move to lighter touch and kissing in between the hard bites.

Scratching

There is nothing like scratching to bring in the animalistic aspects of sexuality. Light scratching is like a form of feather touch and can be very arousing at the beginning of a sexual experience. Her body may need more time to warm up for it to get the most out of deeper scratching or gripping with your nails.

Spanking

Whether your sweetheart is a "good girl" or a "bad girl," if delivered correctly, an intermittent spank can be very erotic. There are entire workshops given about spanking alone and there can be many wonderful nuances to a good spank. Here we offer you our two favorite spanks, which are by far the most arousing and which can be most easily incorporated into any hot sexual experience.

1. **Slapping** – A slapping spank is done with a flat hand and has follow through. Slapping spanks have more of stinging feeling and usually make more noise.

2. **Cupping** – Cup your hand and end the spank at

the butt cheek, do not follow through. Cupping offers more of a deep, pounding feeling.

After the Spank – some people plant a nice slap on their partner's ass and move on to the next spank or another part of the body, missing an amazing opportunity. Immediately after a spank, the blood has moved to the surface of her ass cheek, making the spot where you just spanked a highly sensitized part of the body. Immediately after the slap, give the spot some feathery touch or slow, light scratches, and watch her ass move even higher into the air to receive you.

Pinching

There are only a few places on the body that respond well to pinching. However, the response can be quite exciting so keep pinching on the list, especially for women who like more intense touch on their nipples or ass. If she likes a whole lot of stimulation on her nipples you can also pinch while pulling on her nipples or twisting them. Ask for feedback about pressure, twisting and pulling. Another great place to pinch is at the softest part of her ass cheeks nearest her pussy. Using this pinching during oral sex might take her over the edge of her orgasm.

Combination Touch

Combination touch is when you use one of the holding touches at the same time that you use a feather touch or an intense touch. The reason that combination touch is so powerful is that the grounding of the holding touch allows the arousing stimulation of the other touch to spread and move more in the body. It also helps keep a woman present with her sensation when she is feeling ticklish or distracted. All of the holding touches, including hair holding, waist holding and ass holding, can be fantastic combined with light caresses on another part of her body such as the back of her neck or down the front of her chest and stomach. You can also combine holding touch with intense touch, such as holding her waist while pinching her nipples or grabbing her ass while you bite her neck.

Give Her Orgasms a Hand

Women's capacity for pleasure and orgasms is endless. While this sounds very promising, these possibilities can bring up performance anxiety for many women who worry that they need to have every type of orgasm and be able to ejaculate, etc. Women also fear that they take too long; while men are often trying to hold off on their orgasms as long as possible, women are generally rushing to the finish.

Women worry that men won't appreciate them as sexual partners if they don't have orgasms the way they think men want them to (i.e., during intercourse or without a vibrator) or quickly enough. Throughout history women suffered from sexual oppression and limitation around their orgasms; they were told that something was wrong with them if they couldn't have what Freud referred to as "vaginal orgasms" and that clitoral orgasms were "immature." We invite you to celebrate women for their full potential without putting pressure on them to prove that they can do it all. The pressure merely leads to women faking orgasms, making it even less likely that you learn how to give her pleasure and orgasm. You can support your partner by letting go of the hierarchy of orgasms and appreciating orgasms however and whenever they come in a sexual experience, as well as allowing women to have their choice around orgasm, since some women might not want to orgasm every time they have sex. In this section we discuss the most common types of female orgasm as well as how you can give her a hand and help her achieve them through manual touch.

The three major types of orgasms – clitoral, G-Spot and cervical – each travel across a different set of nerves and therefore create a different sensation in the body. This also means that women can have combination orgasms, where two or three of the neuropathways are being activated. Below, we explore how you can best help her reach each of these different types of orgasm.

Clitoral Orgasms
Studies have shown that up to seventy percent of

woman need some type of clitoral stimulation in order to orgasm. You can generally tell if a woman is clitorally oriented if she clenches and squeezes her muscles to get to orgasm. Some women like direct touch on their clit while many women's clits are very sensitive and need the protection of their clitoral hood, especially when it is first being touched.

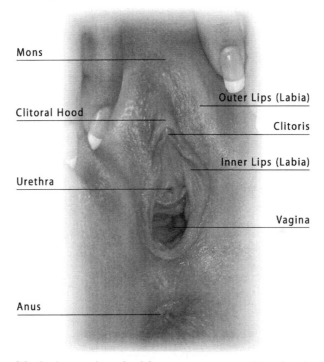

To find out what she likes, you can try asking her how she likes to be touched or ask her to show you how she masturbates. Some women are comfortable with this and some may feel embarrassed. Just because she says no

What is all the fuss about vibrators?

Many women cannot orgasm without a vibrator (or it makes it exponentially easier), yet so many are afraid to bring vibrators to the bedroom. Here are some common reasons why women deny themselves this pleasurable treat:

- They are afraid that they might hurt their partner's ego, fearing he might be thinking "Does this mean that I am not a good enough lover?"
- They fear that something is wrong with them if they need a vibrator to come, so they are willing to forgo orgasms during sex or only have them occasionally.
- They feel (or fear that their partners feel) that vibrators are not "NATURAL."
- They are afraid that they will become addicted to vibrators and not be able to have orgasms through other sexual experiences.

In response, here are some of our personal and professional thoughts about vibrators:

Using a vibrator during sex is as natural as eating with a fork or spoon. If we still did everything "naturally," we'd be living in caves eating raw meat and berries. In the age of electricity and batteries, why not use some BUZZ to make our sex lives more fulfilling? The fact is, we refer to vibrators as man's best friend in bed (the dog may not be much help here)! When using a vibrator, you can also use your hands, fingers, cock, tongue and your words to drive her wild, and

> with the vibrator's help, she can enjoy many orgasms instead of focusing all attention to squeeze one little one out, or worse, to fake one. As for the fear that vibrators might be addictive, studies have shown that this simply is not the case.

once, this does not mean that you should never ask again or find ways to incorporate this into your sex play, relying on non-verbal cues. If she does agree to masturbate in front of you, pay close attention to all of the kinds of touch she is giving to her vulva, including her clitoris and vagina. Notice how she rubs her clit – pay attention especially to the direction, pressure, speed and timing.

To warm up the pussy, teasing, tickling, and holding can be extremely arousing. You can begin holding her whole pussy by cupping your hand so that your middle finger is near her perineum and the palm of your hand is on her mons. After cupping move to feather touch across her entire vulva. This brings us to our second rule to live by: "If it's not wet, don't penetrate it." Women's capacity for lubrication changes throughout their lifetime and their menstrual cycle and, just because they are not wet does not mean they are not aroused. Check with your partner about her lubrication. If she does not lubricate easily on her own, keep a lubricant nearby. Lubricants with a pump spout are best because they are easily accessible.

When first approaching the clit, continue the very light touch. When touching her clit, use the soft pads of at least three of your fingers. Using the soft pads instead of your fingertips give you more coverage making it more likely that you stimulate the most sensitive parts of her clit. When you are still bringing her arousal up, continue to be playful and creative, visiting the clit and then moving away so that the anticipation continues to build. Once she gets close to orgasm (which is often signaled non-verbal through clenching the muscles, holding her breath and/or making sound), stop being creative and continue doing *exactly* what you were doing when she started getting close until she comes.

The Three Basic Moves

Women who masturbate using their hands either move their fingers up and down, side-to-side, or in circles across their pussy. These are the three basic strokes. You can do any of them slowly and lightly using longer strokes, then moving to faster touch and adding pressure as her arousal increases. When you add more pressure and move your hand faster, your strokes may get shorter; still make sure to get a lot of motion across the clit.

Advanced Clit Play

The Taco – If her clit is large enough, you can squeeze her outer lips so that they snuggly surround the clit; this makes the clit pop out a little bit so that you can brush across it lightly with your fingers, stroking from the vagina up to the mons, side to side or in circles.

The Anchor – Anchor two fingers so that one is on either side of the clit in between the inner and outer lips. Move the fingers in very small vibrating motions so that the clit feels the vibration.

Party Time – For many women the two o'clock point or the ten o'clock point on the clit can be very pleasurable due to additional nerve bundling in those locations. You might try focusing your stimulation at these points and see if you get more response.

You might consider introducing a vibrator into your relationship, especially if she needs an extended amount of stimulation, lots of pressure or very quick motions. Finding a good vibrator is a matter of trial and error. We love the Hitachi Magic Wand because of the deep, penetrating vibrations but it is also very strong. Try using a washcloth between her vulva and the vibrator when you first try it and make sure she is very warmed up.

Multiple Orgasms

If a woman is not already multi-orgasmic, she can become multi-orgasmic if she wishes to do so. After the first clitoral orgasm, the clitoris may initially be very sensitive and the last thing a woman wants is for her clitoris to be touched or stimulated in any way. If her clit needs a break after the first orgasm, she will likely give you either verbal or non-verbal cues, which might include closing her legs, pushing you out, or pulling her body away from you. Women who have never experienced multi-orgasms assume that this first orgasm is the end of their sexual journey. They often feel satisfied and don't want to go on.

If she wishes to become multi-orgasmic, cup her clit after her first orgasm by holding her vulva with your entire hand – this helps to ground her. After ten to thirty seconds, her clitoris should lose the intense sensitivity and she can enjoy a new wave of pleasure through clitoral stimulation. Often orgasms after her first orgasm come faster, and can be closer together, which means a lot more payoff for a lot less effort.

G-Spot Orgasms

Some people say that women reach their sexual peak at 40. While this is not hormonally accurate, we believe this might be particularly true for women who discover G-Spot pleasure later in life. G-Spot stimulation can add a whole new level of pleasure to your partner's sex life, substantially increasing her orgasmic potential.

The most important piece of information that you and your partner need to know about the G-Spot is that its capacity for sensation develops throughout a woman's lifetime. Some women believe that they don't have a G-Spot because, when the area is touched, they don't feel immediate sensation or arousal. They may even feel some irritation. This just means that the G-Spot has not yet been developed to its full potential. To awaken the G-Spot, you need to massage it and give it focused stimulation over time.

The G-Spot is located right past the pelvic bone on the upper wall of the vagina. You can locate the G-Spot by placing one or two fingers inside the vagina a bit past the first knuckle and then bending you fingers so that they are saying "come here." You can get a good idea of what it feels like by doing the following: put your tongue on the roof of your mouth right behind your teeth. Feel the bumpy part of the roof of your mouth. If you go a little farther back into your mouth with your tongue, there is a smooth area. Inside the vagina there is a rough area first; this is called the urethral sponge. Deeper inside the vagina, is a smooth area. Pressure from your fingers into the smooth area gives the best G-Spot sensation.

For a small percentage of women, the G-Spot develops early and is naturally where they feel a lot of sensation. However, for many women, the G-Spot has not yet been developed and it can take weeks or sometimes even a year of consistent stimulation for a woman to feel pleasure from it. Unfortunately, because many women have been told that the G-Spot is a myth, when they feel numbness or irritation from G-Spot stimulation, they give up and don't explore the potential pleasure that is there for them.

During penetration, the cock moves across the G-Spot; however, if a G-Spot is not awakened at all, the cock is unlikely to provide enough pressure and stimulation to awaken it. Beginning instead with your fingers has two perks. Firstly, you have access to a wide range of pressure, so you can start gently and slowly work your way up. Secondly, your finger is very sensitive and you can begin to map the locations on or around her G-Spot that are most responsive. Massaging the G-Spot while applying increasing pressure, speed and intensity, and while encouraging the woman to breathe and relax, is the surest way to awaken and arouse the G-Spot.

When massaged patiently, the G-Spot grows and expands, eventually filling with ejaculate. Pressing on it might make your partner feel like she wants to pee. Many women are worried and embarrassed that they might pee on their partner, so they hold back at the most important pre-orgasmic moment, tightening up instead of letting go. This stops them from experiencing the depth of intensity that the G-Spot can provide. If they can open up and let go in this moment, they have the opportunity to have a G-Spot orgasm, and they may also ejaculate at the same time.

While clitoral orgasm generally comes from clenching, G-Spot orgasms are brought on when the woman opens and relaxes her body or pushes down and out as if trying to pee. G-Spot orgasms can be extremely intense and are more likely than clitoral orgasms to spread throughout a woman's whole body.

G-Spot Basics

When exploring your partner's G-Spot, it is essential to warm up her body and pussy. If she commonly has orgasms through clitoral stimulation, give her at least one clitoral orgasm before beginning to explore the G-Spot. Once you begin exploring the G-Spot, the clitoris can become elusive. In your G-Spot explorations, give yourself plenty of time (at least an hour) and let your partner know that she doesn't need to try to orgasm or ejaculate, that she can simply allow herself to be receptive and feel into what sensations are possible for her.

Start slowly and lightly and build speed and pressure slowly – Make sure you try lots of different strokes, speeds and pressures and ask for feedback about what feels best for her. Don't forget, this is likely to change throughout the day, and over the weeks, months and years of her life. As she becomes more aroused, she can generally take more pressure and some women need a lot of pressure to be able to orgasm from their G-Spot, while others respond to lighter touch.

Work your way back – Start with the tip of your finger at the opening of your partner's vagina and make slow circles with your fingers. If she is willing to, have her give you feedback on how it feels and ask her if she wants more or less pressure or speed. Continue with slow circles at the opening, then across the bumpy part and then directly on the G-Spot.

Let her lead – Once you get to the G-Spot you can begin to give it pressure and let her move towards or away from your fingers so she can help you find the right location and pressure.

Come hither – Thrust across the G-Spot with the "come here" motion. Some women like the "come here" motion right on top of the bumpy part while others prefer it on the smoother part right past the pubic bone. Try making quicker "come here" motions with your fingers pulling towards you; if you are on the right spot, you will be able to hook your fingers behind her pubic bone.

Advanced G-Spot Play

Explore the grooves – In addition to stimulation directly on the G-Spot, there are also "grooves" on either side of the urethral sponge. You can slide your fingers along these grooves and you can also squeeze the sponge between your fingers.

Tapping – Insert your fingers and tap directly on the G-Spot. Start gently and work your way up, seeing how much pressure it can take. Vary the speed.

Getting noisy – One way to help a woman to bring more sensation to her G-Spot is to encourage her to make sound while you stimulate her G-Spot; this helps relax the muscles in her vagina and allows her to move towards orgasm. For some women, G-Spot simulation and orgasms can be very emotional; your partner may cry, laugh, or scream. Stay present for whatever comes up, including any emotion that may come up from ecstasy to tears or the combination of both.

Uterine or Cervical Orgasms

One woman said her uterine orgasm felt like someone was ringing a big bell inside of her and she said, "I felt like that bell was still ringing for 3 days afterwards." Cervical orgasms can be extremely intense and are created when your fingers or cock press on or around the cervix. The cervix protrudes into the vagina. You can put pressure directly onto the protruding area or on the moats around the edge of the cervix.

Sometimes women like direct stimulation on or across the cervix, while other women are more aroused when you use your fingers to circle her cervix or give thrusting pressure around the edges in the moats. Often there is one area that is most sensitive though this can also shift and move throughout her cycle and her lifetime.

Combination Orgasms: Any of these orgasms can be combined for a greater intensification of pleasure. Vibrators can be great for combination orgasms. For example, you might stimulate her G-Spot and/or cervix while she uses a vibrator on her clit.

Tease Your Way to the Center

Oral Sex

In combination with the all-over body caressing and warming up that we've described above, oral sex can be a complete sex act in and of itself – either giving, receiving or both. If you have watched plenty of porn, then you have likely had extensive lessons in how NOT to have oral sex. Porn oral sex is for one purpose only – giving the audience a good show through proper camera angle, and to get a good camera angle the giver of the oral sex needs to keep his distance. Great oral sex is about diving in and savoring every moment, so, if you can see it with the camera, you are probably doing it wrong.

While it may be difficult for you to believe, there are actually some women who do not like oral sex. There are essentially two main reasons why a woman might not like oral sex. The first one is that she may feel ashamed or embarrassed about her pussy. She may think that it looks, smells or tastes bad and this may make it difficult for her to relax and enjoy. If she is generally uncomfortable with her body or sex – even if she doesn't tell you why – this is likely the reason. If your partner doesn't like oral sex for this reason, you may be able to help her overcome this embarrassment by telling her how beautiful her pussy is and how delicious it tastes and smells. It might take time.

Avoid pressuring her to receive oral sex, but continue giving her these messages and revisiting her pussy, especially when she is at her highest arousal states. Sometimes when women feel highly aroused, their inhibitions can be lower and this is a good time to help her relax and enjoy the experience. You can also try giving oral stimulation over her panties.

If your partner is comfortable with her body and sexuality, she still might not like oral sex because she is not clit-oriented. Some women orgasm solely from other parts of their body, like their G-Spot, cervix, ass or nipples. You can go down on this type of woman for hours and never get her any closer to an orgasm. If your partner is one of these kinds of women and you *really* love to give oral sex you may be able to negotiate some pussy-licking by telling her that you just want to do it for a while and you'd love for her to relax and enjoy, with no pressure for her to orgasm. Many women who don't come through oral stimulation still find it pleasurable or arousing. You can also incorporate stimulation of her G-Spot, asshole, nipples or cervix and see if it is possible for her to have pleasure during oral sex or even more of a combination orgasm. Also remember that women's comfort, bodies, and desires change throughout their lives so, even if she doesn't want oral sex now, you can occasionally give it a try and see if she changes her mind.

Usually women who like oral sex *like it a lot*, which

means it is important to take your time. Oral sex offers a woman a lot of direct clitoral stimulation, and using your tongue can be a great way to bring her to orgasm. Once you have warmed up her body, you can begin to move towards her pussy, taking your time and lingering on some of the more sensitive areas we discussed, especially the lower part of her stomach and her inner thighs. When you first make contact, keep in mind that it is still all about sensual creativity and teasing.

One excellent transition is to go from kissing her thighs and stomach to bringing light, teasing kisses to her pussy. Because kisses represent love and affection, kissing is a wonderful way to show her pussy how much you desire it and appreciate it while continuing the tease. Cover her whole pussy with soft kisses, including her mons and lips, being very gentle near the clit. Remember, you can always move to more direct and heavy pressure later, but if you bring it in too quickly you miss an opportunity to make her crazy with your teases. Another wonderful approach to teasing is to think of her pussy as a delicious peach ice cream cone. Keep your tongue soft, wide and flat, just like you would if you were licking ice cream and begin with long, slow, light, sensual licks from the bottom of the pussy to the top. Aside from the ice-cream cone lick, you can also suck gently or more vigorously on her outer lips or her inner lips if they are large enough. Also try gliding your tongue between her inner and outer lips before you bring direct touch and pressure to her clit.

Don't get lost in the pussy. Sometimes the pussy can feel like a world in and of itself and it is possible to get lost there and to forget about the other parts of her body. Continued manual touch on her thighs, stomach, breast and nipples can heighten sensation and pleasure and help bring her to orgasm. Try stroking her hips, pinching her nipples or adding in G-Spot stimulation to increase her overall sensation.

Once you do move to the clit, the basic strokes are up and down, side-to-side or circles. Begin slowly and slowly increase the speed and pressure throughout the experience. Pay attention to her non-verbal cues. If she is pulling her pelvis away from you, she likely needs lighter pressure, while grabbing your head or pushing her pelvis towards you is likely a sign she needs more pressure. An important cue is how she is moving her hips. Sadly, for women it is sometimes still difficult to simply say "a little to the left." Instead, women move their hips a little to the right, hoping you will stay put. Some men are so engrossed in what they are doing, they follow the pussy around wherever it goes, and miss this non-verbal cue completely. If she is moving to the left, she needs you to be more to the right; if she's moving her hips up, she needs you lower down on her clit; and she is moving her hips down, she needs your tongue higher on her clit. If

Anal Play – The Final Frontier

There's a joke among sex therapists:

Question: "How many times do women usually have anal sex?"

Answer: "Once."

Yep, that's the whole joke, but every sex therapist gets the joke because anal sex done badly is really painful and most anal sex is not done well. The saddest part about it is that anal play of all kinds can be extremely pleasurable for women (and men for that matter) but most people have so many taboos, fears or bad experiences that folks don't even try it. For some women, anal touch, oral-anal stimulation (sometimes called "rimming") or light or full anal penetration (with a finger for example), is one very helpful way to more deeply arouse and engage the clitoris, and anal play can help some women get over the edge of orgasm. The first rule of anal play is to use tons of lube. The anus is not self-lubricating so purchase lube – spit or her natural vaginal lubrication is not enough for her to have a truly delightful experience.

There are two great ways to initiate anal play, depending on how communicative your partner is. If she likes to talk, bring it up and let her share her stance on it. Let her have her feelings about it and don't try to talk her out of them – just listen and make space for them. If she gets really embarrassed by sexual topics, test the waters during oral play by slowly and gently stroking her anus externally. If she stays relaxed, stay there and play, continuing to play with the edge of her boundaries until you find them. If she tightens up or pulls away, you need to have a conversation if you want anything more to happen.

This brings us to another rule to live by: "If it goes in the ass, it doesn't go in the pussy." Make sure you use a different finger if you are going to stimulate her ass and her pussy in the same sexual encounter, and if you want to have anal and then vaginal intercourse either use a condom for anal or wash very well in between; if not, she might get a yeast infection, which is no fun!

she is behaving like a bucking bronco and you can't seem to keep connected with her clit, just keep your tongue flat and available and let her rub herself across it.

There are some great variations you can bring to the picture by adding anchoring, suction and light nibbling and biting. If her clitoral shaft is big enough, you can anchor her clit by wrapping your lips around it so that you can hold it in place. When you have it anchored with your lips, lick the clit with up-and-down, side-to-side or circular motions. Anchoring the shaft of her clit gives increased sensation because both the sides of her clitoral shaft and the head of her clit are getting stimulation. From the anchored position, you can also add light suction to the mix, sucking the clit in between your lips, then releasing and sucking again. You can also move your lips up and down across the shaft, kind of like a clitoral blowjob. Suction pulls more blood into the clit and can really increase sensation. You can also try nibbling lightly with your teeth or running your teeth lightly up and down her clitoral shaft.

As she gets closer to coming, she will usually breathe faster, and may even help you out with words such as "Don't stop," "I'm going to cum" or "Yes, just like that." At this point, you need to completely let go of creativity, allow her to get you to the right location and pressure, and keep doing *exactly what you are doing*. Women's orgasms can be elusive creatures – a slight change in rhythm, direction or pressure at this moment and you may have to go all the way back to the start. No matter what she does, if she is bucking, squeezing your face or suffocating you, as long as you aren't going to die, just keep doing what you are doing until you feel her release.

During oral sex, some women like to have a finger in their vagina, their asshole or both for increased pleasure and sensation and the potential for combination orgasms. Women who orgasm solely from their clit might be distracted by the insertion of a finger. If she pulls away when you try to insert a finger, stops making sounds or seems to relax her body and move away from orgasm, take your finger back out. For those women who do like it, manual G-Spot, cervical or anal stimulation can be extremely pleasing in combination with oral sex and may be just what they need to take them to the heights or bring them over the edge. Don't forget to use different fingers for the asshole and the vagina so as not to cause a yeast infection and use lube for anal insertion. To introduce a finger, take it slow; at first simply tease your fingers over her asshole or over the lips of her vagina. Later, try inserting a finger into her vagina, her ass or both. Whether you are in her ass or vagina, you can try hooking your fingers up and giving her the "come here" motion to stimulate her G-Spot or thrust your fingers in and out to give her more of a "fucking" feeling. If you go all the way into her vagina during oral sex, you can also stimulate her on or around her cervix. All of these bring in the possibility of increased pleasure and sensation and combination orgasms.

Intercourse

If you take the time to warm up her whole body, you prime her for tremendous pleasure during intercourse, whether she can orgasm during intercourse or not. If a woman's body is not warmed up, she is much less likely to orgasm during intercourse or to feel much of anything at all.

Some women can and will tell you whether or not they can come during intercourse, and how you need to have sex with them in order to get them there. Other women fake pleasure and orgasm, making it nearly impossible for you to learn how to really bring them there. Finally, some women give non-verbal cues and clues with their body, which you can read in order to figure out the best ways to take them there.

If, during oral sex or manual sex, you have found that your partner's orgasms are more clit focused, then use sexual positions that bring your pelvic area right above your cock into consistent contact with her clit. The best positions for this are missionary position and woman-on-top. If she is clit focused, make sure that you are deep inside of her a lot of the time so that your pelvis is making contact with her clit. If you happen to know how she masturbates, this can give you another hint about whether she is more likely to come when she is on top of you or underneath you. If she masturbates lying on her back and needs to clench her muscles a lot, she probably prefers missionary. If she masturbates on her stomach, grinding into her hand or a pillow, she's more likely to come from being on top. And remember, even if she needs it slow and deep to be able to orgasm, she may also really enjoy the sensation of hard and fast to turn her on or warm her up.

Some women can only come during intercourse using their hand or a vibrator. If this is the case, try positions that give her room to get her hand or a vibrator in there. A modified missionary position where you are sitting upright (she may need a pillow under her butt for this) or in a push-up can both work well. She can also touch herself if she is on top of you in a cowgirl position, and doggie style can be a great position for her to incorporate a vibrator of any size.

If she is more G-Spot oriented, it is important to remember that the G-Spot generally needs a lot of pressure. Use positions that point your cock directly towards her G-Spot. One of the best positions for G-Spot stimulation is the modified missionary position, where the woman is lying on her back and you are kneeling in front of her. This way your cock points upwards toward the G-Spot and giving it direct stimulation and a lot of pressure. The other great position is woman-on-top, where the woman is leaning back slightly so that she gets a lot of pressure on her G-Spot. The other great thing about women-on-top is that she can also stimulate her clitoris with her hand or alternate leaning forward and backwards and getting additional clitoral stimulation that way. This increases your likelihood of a combination orgasm.

Doggie style can give G-Spot stimulation and is also a great position for women who come from their cervix, as it allows you to get as deep as you can into their pussy. Make sure you experiment with different angles. If you find an angle that she really responds to, stick with it. Adding clitoral stimulation can create a great combination cervical-clit orgasm.

Finally, most sexual encounters follow a predictable trajectory - kissing, touching, oral sex (maybe), then intercourse that continues uninterrupted until the man orgasms. Both men and women think of male orgasm as the obvious end of every sexual experience. This insinuates that everything else that happens during sex is just a warm up for the main event – men's orgasm. For a much more varied and playful sex life, try switching it up. For example, oral or manual sex can be more exciting for some women after they have already been penetrated. Many women are capable of a few more orgasms once you have already come. By breaking the expectation that sex ends with your orgasm, you will be a standout among men.

EXERCISE
Sensual Sex – Putting it All Together

Now it is time for you to practice putting all of the pieces together. To help you do this, we have included a story that a woman from one of our Women's Workshops wrote about her hottest sexual experience. This story highlights all of the qualities and techniques you have learned in this book and puts them into a single, mind-blowing sexual experience. Remember, women describe their experiences in a narrative form – one that builds with passion and intensity. After the story, we point out some significant parts.

The way he looked at me sent shivers up my spine. He was standing slightly apart from me and running his eyes slowly up and down my body with a piercing look. He ran his eyes from my eyes to my lips, contouring my neck, adoring my breasts, tracing the shape of my hips. Just through his look, I already felt like he was taking me.

He approached me slowly and I felt both mesmerized and paralyzed. He began to touch my face and my hair, looking in my eyes, then kissing me. He gently took off my clothes and moved me towards the bed. He continued to kiss my lips and caress my body softly while his eyes held me entranced. Every part that he touched on my body filled with electricity. He traced his hands up and down my sides, and each kiss he gave me was more passionate then the next. I felt our desire building together. He kneeled in front of me, spread my legs and just looked at my pussy, telling me not to move. I got immediately wet just from his eyes admiring my pussy. I could tell how delicious he thought I was.

He pulled his hard cock out of his pants and said, "You know how much I love to look at your pussy. It makes me so hard." He teased me slowly with his tongue, licking my inner thighs and moaning with pleasure. He spread my pussy lips with his tongue and licked them softly, barely touching my clit. He continued to tease my pussy with his tongue but not enough to bring me to orgasm. He played with my nipples while he licked me then ran his tongue towards my stomach, circled my nipples and kissed me passionately.

As I felt him enter me, I had the sense that I was being completely taken over, filled by his breath, his kisses, and his cock. His hands continued to grab at my ass and thighs as he moved in and out. It felt like he was going deeper and deeper inside me with every thrust. He pulled out of me and put two large fingers inside of my pussy reaching towards my G-Spot. I felt this delicious sensation of being both taken and taken care of, of trusting him to know what he is doing.

I felt a rush of energy and tingling all over my body. A warmth and intensity spread from my pussy to my stomach to my throat and my face began to flush. He looked in my eyes and thrust his fingers inside me, telling me how much he loved to feel the wetness on his hands. I felt him thrusting harder and harder, looking at me and shaking with intensity, telling me, "I want to take it from you."

I felt an intense orgasm, which began in my pussy and spread through my body. My nipples got harder and I felt the orgasm move up the center of my body to my throat. I heard a woman screaming with pleasure and I realized it was me. I looked down and he was drinking the flood coming from my pussy and spreading it across his chest. From the intense look he was giving me, I knew he would drink me like that forever.

All of the 9 Qualities of an Extraordinary Lover can be found in this story. Notice the importance of **presence** through eye contact and connection, as well as the **passion** he brings when he looks at her and touches her. You can feel the intensity of his words as well as the **sensuality** of his touch, as he moves from slow, to teasing, to more aggressive touch. He is **curious** about and **accepts** all of her, spreading her lips to look at her pussy and drinking her ejaculate. He is **spontaneous**, creatively using every tool to give her pleasure and he is flexibly abandoning the normal trajectory by going from intercourse to manual sex. He is **generous** and delighted by her pleasure and her body's responses, wanting more and more of her and **empathically** feeling her pleasure in his body (as seen by his physical shaking). One of the most significant lines in the story is when she says, "I felt both taken and taken care of." He is **confidently** taking charge and focusing all of his passion on her, thus she feels fully taken and consumed by him. At the same time, his interest in her pleasure and his unwavering presence is a way of taking care of her.

Congratulations!

ongratulations, you made it! You are now a *Cockfident* man and an Extraordinary Lover. You engage your full erotic power and women respond to you with desire. By being the man you want to be, you create a life of pleasure, satisfaction and inspiration. You have gotten out of your head and into your body. You listen to your emotions and accept yourself for who you are. You are now the master of your sexual function and can give generously within your boundaries. You see yourself as equal to others and people trust you because you show up as your authentic self. You feel comfortable with your desires and feel free to engage in experiences that make you feel passionate and alive.

By continuing to live life through the 9 Qualities of an Extraordinary Lover, you emerge every day as the most magnetic, exciting, powerful manifestation of yourself. You understand women's desires and approach your partner with open curiosity. You know how to seduce, tantalize and satisfy your partner with exhilarating experiences that will last a lifetime. You offer the woman in your life empathy and support, while realizing it is not your job to make her happy. By letting go of the responsibility of making her happy, you are free to be fully present and inspired by all that she is. You love her and desire her whether she is joyful, sad, excited or angry. If your partner is ready, she can now open to you completely, sharing her love, passion, desire, and intensity and supporting you in being the full expression of who you are.

Your *Cockfidence* goes beyond your connection with yourself and with women; you exude it everywhere you go. In your career and in life your ideas and presence garner respect and you attract the people and experiences that you most desire and enjoy.

Enjoy your Cockfidence
xoxo,
Celeste & Danielle

Now What?

L ike building muscle, *Cockfidence* is an ongoing process; you decide how much you'd like these muscles to strengthen and gain definition. If you feel inspired to take your *Cockfidence* to the next level and want some personal training and experiential practice in this area, we invite you to try our one-day *Become an Extraordinary Lover Workshop*, where you will practice hands-on the 9 Qualities of an Extraordinary Lover and receive helpful, personal feedback to hone your skills. You can also come for a *Men's Erotic Intensive* or *Individual Coaching* where you master your sexual function and explore your sexual desires, delve into your fantasies, expand pleasure in your body and experience the vitality and motivation of erotic power. You and your partner might try *A Passionate Vacation* or *Couple's Therapy* where you will deepen your sexual connection, increase passion and communication and learn how to move past difficult roadblocks in your relationship. We have offices in San Francisco and

Silicon Valley and also travel to work with clients.

Find us on the Web at: **www.CelesteAndDanielle.com**
Email us: **info@CelesteAndDanielle.com**.

We'd love to play with you!

21114345R00155

Made in the USA
San Bernardino, CA
07 May 2015